PERFECT
ENDING

WHY YOUR FUTURE
MATTERS TODAY

OTHER BOOKS BY ROBERT JEFFRESS

Twilight's Last Gleaming

How Can I Know?

PERFECT ENDING

WHY YOUR FUTURE MATTERS TODAY

ROBERT JEFFRESS

WORTHY
PUBLISHING

Worthy
Hachette Book Group
1290 Avenue of the Americas, New York, NY 10104
worthypublishing.com
twitter.com/worthypub

First Edition: February 2014

Worthy is a division of Hachette Book Group, Inc. The Worthy name and logo are trademarks of Hachette Book Group, Inc.

The publisher is not responsible for websites (or their content) that are not owned by the publisher.

Published in association with Yates & Yates, www.yates2.com

Unless otherwise noted, Scripture quotations are taken from the NEW AMERICAN STANDARD BIBLE®, Copyright © 1960, 1962, 1963, 1968, 1971, 1972, 1973, 1975, 1977, 1995 by The Lockman Foundation. Used by permission. | Scripture quotations marked NIV are taken from THE HOLY BIBLE, NEW INTERNATIONAL VERSION®, NIV® Copyright © 1973, 1978, 1984, 2011 by Biblica, Inc.® Used by permission. All rights reserved worldwide.

Cover Design by Scott Williams | Richmond & Williams. Cover Image © Bateleur | Crestock.

Print book interior design by ThinkpenDesign.com.

Jeffress, Robert, 1955-
Perfect ending / Robert Jeffress.
pages cm
Includes bibliographical references and index.
ISBN 978-1-61795-183-1 (pbk.)
1. End of the world. I. Title.
BT877.J44 2014
236'.9--dc23

ISBN: 9781683970484 (paperback)

Printed in the United States of America

LSC-C

CONTENTS

1. Why Study Bible Prophecy? 11

2. It Begins and Ends with Israel 29

3. Getting the Big Picture 49

4. Not Left Behind 65

5. When All Hell Breaks Loose 89

6. History's Most Important Event 119

7. Heaven on Earth 137

8. Final Judgment 161

9. Rewards in Heaven 181

10. The Truth about Eternity 201

Study Questions 225

Notes 233

Chapter One

||||||||||||||||||||||||||||||||||||||||||

WHY STUDY
BIBLE PROPHECY?

Have you ever read the novel *Futility, or the Wreck of the Titan* by Morgan Robertson? The novella tells the story of a magnificent ocean liner named the *Titan* that strikes an iceberg on its maiden voyage from Southampton to New York and sinks in the middle of the ocean. You are probably thinking, "This sure does sound like the real story of the *Titanic*." Yet Robertson's novel differs from the actual event in several ways. The ship in *Futility* was 1,800 feet long while the real *Titanic* was 1,882 feet long. The *Titan* was able to displace 66,000 tons of water, while the *Titanic* was able to displace 70,000 tons of water. Yet both ships were triple-screw ocean liners that could travel up to twenty-five knots per hour and transport three thousand passengers.

You might wonder why Morgan Robertson would bother to write a novella that so closely approximated a real-life event. And why go to the trouble of varying some of the facts ever so slightly including the name of the ship: *Titan* versus *Titanic*? The reason is quite simple. The *Titanic* sank on April 14, 1912. The novel *Futility* was published in 1898—fourteen years before the actual event![1]

It is amazing to think that a book written more than a decade earlier could so accurately forecast a historical event like the sinking of the *Titanic*. But it is even more fascinating to realize that the Bible is able to foretell with laser-like accuracy events that will occur hundreds and even thousands of years after it was written. One can hardly turn a page of Scripture without finding some reference to a future event. Yet, in spite of the large amount of space devoted to prophetic themes, few Christians have a clear understanding of the events that will lead to the return of Jesus Christ. Maybe you are one of those Christians who:

- reaches for Tylenol when your "Read Through the Bible" plan lands you in the book of Daniel;
- thinks about changing churches when your pastor announces a year-long study in the book of Revelation;
- breaks out in a cold sweat if a new Christian asks you to briefly explain the terms "Rapture," "Tribulation," and "Millennium";
- wonders why you should purchase this book instead of *Seven Scintillating Secrets for a Sensual Marriage*.

WHY PEOPLE RESIST STUDYING PROPHECY

Evangelist Billy Graham once observed that "the most neglected teaching in the church today is the second coming of Jesus Christ."[2] Why is that? As I have talked with both pastors and laymen about prophecy I have discovered four major objections to studying Bible prophecy:

1. "The subject is too confusing to understand."

Most Christians are convinced that you must possess a seminary degree (or at least some skill in reading tea leaves) to comprehend the events surrounding the return of Jesus Christ. Not long ago I was visiting with the pastor of one of the largest churches in the denomination in which I serve (Southern Baptist). This man has an earned ThD from a respected seminary and preaches to thousands of people each week. He said, "Robert, would you please write a simple book explaining Bible prophecy so that people like me can understand it?" If this doctor of theology feels inadequate to understand prophecy, it's no wonder that thousands in his congregation will never hear a series of messages on books of the Bible like Daniel and Revelation.

One of my closest friends is convinced that God never meant for us to understand prophecy: "If God really wanted us to understand these things, why didn't He make them clearer in Scripture?" My response is, "God *has* clearly explained end time events in Scripture." As an example I have directed his attention to Matthew 24–25.

As Jesus and His disciples were leaving the temple, Jesus remarked that one day every stone of that magnificent place of worship would be torn down. Obviously shaken at such a statement (How would you respond if someone told you that one day the church you attend would be completely leveled?), the disciples asked the obvious question: "Tell us, when will these things happen, and what will be the sign of Your coming, and of the end of the age?" (Matthew 24:3).

We know from history that about forty years after the disciples' question, the Roman conqueror Titus entered Jerusalem and destroyed the temple. But it is clear from their question that this is not the only event with which they were concerned. They also wanted to know when Christ would return and what signs would precede His return and the end of the age. Notice what Jesus did *not* say in reply to their inquiry: "Boys, there is no way you could understand these events—especially you, Peter!"

Or, "This is nothing you need to concern yourselves with. Trust me. Everything will pan out in the end."

Or, "You shouldn't care about the end-time events. All you should be concerned with is sharing the gospel with as many people as possible."

Instead, Jesus answered the disciples' question with a lengthy explanation concerning end-time events. Although Jesus refused to answer the question "when" (in verse 36, Jesus confessed that even *He* did not know when these events would occur), He clearly answered "what" will happen:

And Jesus answered and said to them, "See to it that no one misleads you. For many will come in My name, saying, 'I am the Christ,' and will mislead many. You will be hearing of wars and rumors of wars. See that you are not frightened, for those things must take place, but that is not yet the end . . . Therefore when you see the Abomination of Desolation which was spoken of through Daniel the prophet, standing in the holy place (let the reader understand), then those who are in Judea must flee to the mountains . . . But immediately after the tribulation of those days the Sun will be darkened, and the moon will not give its light, and the stars will fall from the sky, and the powers of the heavens will be shaken. And then the sign of the Son of Man will appear in the sky, and then all the tribes of the earth will mourn, and they will see the Son of Man coming on the clouds of the sky with power and great glory. (Matthew 24:4–6, 15–16, 29–30)

In chapter 3 we will discover that Matthew 24–25 gives us a very simple outline of the end-time events that includes the Great Tribulation, the return of Christ, the judgments, and Christ's thousand-year rule on the earth.

2. "No one can know when Christ will return."

Bill and Janet are friends of ours who keep up with the latest fads in eschatology (a word describing the study of end-time events). Years ago they took seriously Edgar Whisenant's prediction that the Rapture (an event explained in the next chapter) was slated for 1988. However, they decided to prepare for this event in a most unusual way. They drained their savings account, loaded their van, and headed for—not the Millennial Kingdom—but the Magic Kingdom in Orlando, Florida.

I will admit that their response to the return of Christ is unique; nevertheless, it illustrates one reason so many people are skeptical about a study of the end times. Bible prophecy "experts" have turned a lot of people off of the subject of studying the end times by violating a very basic principle in the Scripture: we are never to set dates concerning the Second Coming of Christ. No one knows the date any prophetic event will occur. For example, the Old Testament prophet Daniel did not know when the end would come:

"He [the angel of the Lord] said, 'Go your way, Daniel, for these words are concealed and sealed up until the end time'" (Daniel 12:9).

Although the apostle Paul probably thought he would live to see the end-time events unfold, he confessed that the Day of the Lord would come unexpectedly:

"Now as to the times and the epochs, brethren, you have no need of anything to be written to you. For you yourselves know full well that the day of the Lord will come just like a thief in the night" (1 Thessalonians 5:2).

While on earth, even Jesus Christ Himself admitted that He had no idea when He would return:

"But of that day and hour no one knows, not even the angels of heaven, nor the Son, but the Father alone" (Matthew 24:36).

If the prophet Daniel, the apostle Paul, and Jesus Christ could not give a date for the end of time, you would think that would discourage others from doing so. Think again. History is filled with those who have made false predictions about when the end of the world would occur:

- Christopher Columbus (1451–1506) thought the world would end in 1656: "There are but 155 years left . . . at which time . . . the world will come to an end," Columbus prophesied.
- Martin Luther (1483–1546) didn't think the world could exist past three hundred years from his time.
- The psychic Edgar Cayce (1877–1945) predicted the Second Coming of Jesus Christ in 2000.

In more recent years radio preacher Harold Camping falsely predicted that the Rapture (the removal of all Christians from the earth prior to the Great Tribulation, an event that will be discussed in chapter 4) would occur on September 6, 1994; September 29, 1994; October 4, 1994; and on March 31, 1995. With a track record of four failed predictions, he next predicted the Rapture and the Judgment Day would take place on May 21, 2011, with the world coming to an end on October 21, 2011. In March 2012, Camping admitted that he had erred and planned to research the Bible more fervently to correct his previous mistaken predictions. As my daughters are fond of saying, "Thank you, Captain Obvious!"

At the end of 2012, the world focused on the Mayan calendar, which abruptly ended with the entry of December 21, 2012. People around the world panicked that this could signal the end of the world, causing NASA to release a video in early December 2012 reassuring the world's population that the planet would survive beyond the so-called Doomsday.

In a column for CNN Belief Blog, I noted that the problem with all of these false predictions is that they discourage people from making the necessary preparation for the real event when it actually occurs. Remember the boy who cried wolf once too often? The villagers were so hardened to the boy's false alarms that they were unprepared when the wolf finally arrived.

Make no mistake about it, the end *is* coming, but God has not told us when—and for good reason. Just as every teacher knows how unproductive and unfocused students are the week before school lets out, God knows how tempted we would be to neglect the responsibilities He has entrusted to us if we knew the date for the end of the world or the end of our life here on earth. That is why God refuses to show us His calendar and instead instructs us to focus on our assignment.

So, if it is impossible to know when major prophetic events will unfold, why bother to study Bible prophecy at all? Not long ago, I arrived at the Los Angeles airport late in the evening and needed a shuttle to take me to my hotel. I called the shuttle service and asked when the next van would be available to transport me to the hotel. Although they could not tell me when the van would arrive, they told me what to watch for: a blue van marked "SkyLark" that had a sign reading "Wilshire." During the next twenty minutes many vans stopped in front of the loading zone . . . orange vans, white vans, red vans. There were even a number of blue SkyLark vans with signs reading "Disneyland" or "Hollywood." Had I boarded any of those vans I would not have arrived safely at my destination. However, eventually the right van with the right sign arrived, and I knew to get on. Why? Even though I had not been told when, I had been told what to look for.

In the same way, none of us knows when the Lord will return. Nevertheless, God has given us a clear indication of what to look for so that we will not be deceived by those false Christs that have appeared in every generation and would lead us in the wrong direction.

3. "There are too many different interpretations of prophecy for the subject to be that important."

Some time ago I was on a panel answering questions about theology. On the panel with me was a well-known speaker and author on the subject of apologetics. When someone asked a question concerning prophecy, he said, "I'd better let Robert answer this one. You see, I am not a premillennialist, postmillennialist, or an amillennialist. I am a panmillennialist. I believe everything will 'pan' out in the end." Chuckle, chuckle.

Granted, there are a number of differing interpretations concerning the end-time events. If you have been confused by terms like "premillennialist," "postmillennialist," and "amillennialist," or "Pretribulation Rapture" and "Posttribulation Rapture," this book will help you to understand these often confusing terms. Nevertheless, the fact that there are a number of different interpretations about end-time events does not mean there is not one correct interpretation.

Perhaps you just cringed when you read that phrase "one correct interpretation." That's understandable. We live in an age where anyone who claims his or her interpretation to be the correct interpretation is viewed with suspicion and disdain. How many times have you heard people say that "everyone is free to interpret the Bible as he chooses"? That statement is true—but only partially. While everyone has the freedom to draw his or her own conclusions about the Bible, not everyone's interpretation is equally valid—especially when it involves the subject of Bible prophecy. Consider the words of the apostle Peter:

"But know this first of all, that no prophecy of Scripture is *a matter of one's own* interpretation [emphasis mine], for no prophecy was ever made by an act of human will, but men moved by the Holy Spirit spoke from God" (2 Peter 1:20–21).

Don't allow the variety of opinions concerning prophecy to cause you to throw up your hands in despair (Can you think of any truth in the Bible about which *everyone* agrees?). Although many of the details about end-time events are concealed and, therefore, open to speculation, the Bible gives us a clear outline of the events that will lead to the return of Christ.

4. "Bible prophecy has nothing to do with everyday life."

Admittedly, most people are not nearly as concerned with the beast described in Revelation 13 as they are with the beast for which they work five days a week at the office. Trying to make it through one jam-packed week of work, soccer practices, homework, and church activities is difficult enough without trying to figure out the mystery of the seventy weeks described in Daniel 9. Why should I worry about some future Tribulation when I have plenty of my own problems right now?

Yet, knowing where we are going in the future should greatly impact how we live in the present. For example, the highway department in our state decided to construct a major double-deck expressway through the center of a city where I once pastored. Although they did not announce when they will begin the project, all of the restaurant owners and small businesses that lined that highway began selling their property and relocating. Why? The new thoroughfare would eventually reroute traffic away from their establishments, ensuring their demise if they remained. Even though these small businesses did not know when these future events would transpire, the fact that it was going to happen demanded immediate action.

The same principle applies to biblical prophecy. God has clearly revealed what awaits earth and all of her inhabitants. A major reconstruction project is guaranteed. The certainty of the return of Christ, the destruction of the present earth, and every person's individual judgment by God should motivate us to action *now*.

WHY BIBLE PROPHECY IS IMPORTANT

Hopefully you have discovered some answers to the objections you have heard from others (or may have had yourself) to studying Bible prophecy. But you may still be wondering why you should invest both your money and your time in a book like this.

1. Bible prophecy is a major theme in the Bible.

In Bible study there is a principle referred to as "The Law of Proportion." This law simply says that you can tell the importance of a certain subject in Scripture by how much space is devoted to it. Applying this principle to prophecy, we discover that more than one-fourth of the Bible is predictive prophecy. In the Old Testament there are over eighteen hundred references to the return of Christ. Of the 260 chapters in the New Testament, there are more than three hundred references to the Lord's return—one out of every thirty verses. Twenty-three of the twenty-seven New Testament books give prominence to this subject. For every prophecy in Scripture concerning the first coming of Christ, there are eight on Christ's second coming.

Both the proportion and prominence of the prophetic theme in Scripture argue for its importance.

2. An understanding of prophecy helps us to interpret and apply the Bible accurately.

A knowledge of end-time events gives us a framework upon which to hang the rest of Scripture. I believe that it is impossible to properly interpret and apply the Bible without a basic understanding of prophecy. Let me illustrate what I mean by looking at a passage from the Old Testament prophet Isaiah:

> No longer will there be in it an infant who lives but a few days,
> Or an old man who does not live out his days;

> For the youth will die at the age of one hundred
> And the one who does not reach the age of one hundred
> Will be thought accursed. (Isaiah 65:20)

What period of time is in view here when there will be no infant mortality and people will live to be one hundred years of age? Obviously, this was not true in Isaiah's lifetime or in ours. Today infants die daily and only a few adults live to have their centennial birthdays announced on *The Today Show*.

Some might believe that Isaiah is describing life in heaven. Yet, Isaiah says that people will die after the age of one hundred. Will there be death in heaven? Revelation 21:4 promises that in heaven "there will no longer be any death."

So if Isaiah is not referring to our life now or our life in heaven, what period of time is in view here? Isaiah was looking forward to Christ's rule on earth during a period we call the *Millennium*, described in numerous Old Testament and New Testament prophecies. As we will see in future chapters, this will be a unique time in world history when Christ will be reigning from David's throne in Jerusalem for one thousand years. Although it is difficult to comprehend, some believers during this period will possess their resurrection bodies, but other believers (the Tribulation saints) will enter the Millennium in the natural bodies and be subject to death (we will discuss this more completely in chapter 8). It is this period of time that Isaiah is describing. Yet, without a basic understanding of the Millennium it is impossible to comprehend this prophecy.

A basic understanding of Bible prophecy not only helps us to interpret the Bible correctly, but also to apply it accurately. Consider these familiar words of Jesus Christ:

> "For I was hungry, and you gave me something to eat; I was thirsty, and you gave Me something to drink; I was a stranger, and you invited Me in; naked, and you clothed Me; I was sick, and you visited Me; I was in prison, and you came to Me." Then the righteous will answer Him, "Lord, when did we see You hungry, and feed You, or thirsty, and give You something to drink?" . . . The King will answer and say to them, "Truly I say to you, to the extent that you did it to one of these brothers of Mine, even the least of them, you did it to Me." (Matthew 25:35–40)

How many times have you heard someone quote this passage and then make the application that the purpose of the Church is to feed the hungry, clothe the naked, and visit the lonely? Last year our church opened our new $130 million church campus in downtown Dallas. Having led church building programs before, I prepared our congregation for the predictable criticism that would come not only from unbelievers, but from Christians as well: "Think of all the hungry people you could have fed with that money." I reminded our congregation that when Mary anointed Jesus' feet with expensive perfume, a man in the room objected, saying, "Lord, that perfume could have been sold and the money given to the poor" (paraphrased from John 12:5). The man's name was Judas Iscariot.

Jesus' reply to Judas is one you don't often hear quoted: "You always have the poor with you . . ." (John 12:8). Jesus was not indifferent toward the plight of the disadvantaged in society, but He was reminding us that God is interested in more than just meeting the physical needs of people. God is also concerned with satisfying our spiritual needs, and He has charged the Church with that unique responsibility. Every other organization in society—including our massive government—is focused on addressing people's physical needs. Only the Church of Jesus Christ is dedicated to meeting people's spiritual needs.

If that is true, how are we to understand Jesus' words in Matthew 25 about our treatment of the hungry, unclothed, and imprisoned? As you study the context of these verses you discover that they are part of the Olivet Discourse that actually begins in Matthew 24 and describe the events that will lead to the return of Christ. In Matthew 25:31–45, Jesus explains the standard by which He will judge those who survive the Tribulation when He returns. They will be judged by how they treated the 144,000 Jewish witnesses during the Tribulation. For a person living in the Tribulation to clothe, feed, or comfort one of these witnesses would be a sign of his salvation since it would be tantamount to ministering to Christ Himself.

Even though these verses refer to a specific group of people living in a future period of time, Christians freely rip these verses out of context and attempt to apply them to the Church today. While ministering to those who are hurting is both noble and Christlike, it is not the primary mission of the Church. God intended the Church to be more—much more—than a sanctified relief agency.

An understanding of prophecy is necessary to interpret and apply the Bible correctly.

3. An understanding of Bible prophecy motivates us toward godly living.

The Bible never divorces prophetic truth from practical application. In 2 Peter 3, the apostle describes the return of Christ, the destruction of the earth, and the creation of a new heaven and a new earth. But then he adds these words:

"Since all these things are to be destroyed in this way, what sort of people ought you to be in holy conduct and godliness, looking for and hastening the coming of the day of God" (2 Peter 3:11–12).

In *World Aflame*, Billy Graham tells of an incident when former President Dwight Eisenhower was vacationing in Denver a number of years ago and his attention was drawn to an open letter in a local newspaper. Six-year-old Paul Haley, dying of cancer, had expressed a wish to see the president of the United States.

Spontaneously, in one of those gracious gestures remembered long after a president's speeches are forgotten, the president decided to grant the boy's request. One Sunday morning in August a big limousine pulled up outside the Haley home and out stepped the president of the United States. Eisenhower walked up to the door and knocked. Mr. Donald Haley, the father, opened the door. He was wearing blue jeans, an old shirt, and a day's growth of beard. Behind him was little Paul. Their amazement at finding President Eisenhower on their doorstep could hardly be imagined.

"Paul," said the president, "I understand you wanted to see me. I'm glad to see you, Paul." The president shook Paul's hand and the two walked together and conversed for a while. They shook hands again, and the president departed.

The Haleys and their neighbors talked about this kind and thoughtful deed of the president for years afterward. Only one person was not entirely happy about it—Mr. Haley. He could never forget how he was dressed when he opened the door.

"Old jeans, that faded shirt, my unshaven face. What a way to greet the president of the United States," he lamented.

I can tell you something even more embarrassing than that. One day the sky will part, the trumpet will sound, and Jesus Christ will suddenly appear. Unfortunately, many Christians will not be properly "dressed" for His return. They will be wrapped up in the faded clothes of materialism, immorality, and personal ambition instead of the bright linen clothes of righteousness described in Revelation 19:8.

Let me ask you a very personal question. If the Lord were to return today, would you be embarrassed by the appearance of your life? If so, I pray that this study of the end times will be a powerful incentive for you to clothe yourself in holy conduct and godliness as we look forward to His certain return.

Chapter Two

||||||||||||||||||||||||||||||||||||||||||

IT BEGINS AND ENDS WITH ISRAEL

I magine that a friend says, "John Grisham's new novel is the best book I have ever read. You must get a copy and read it immediately." Taking your friend's advice, you purchase Grisham's latest lawyer tale and, after the kids are tucked in bed, sit down in your favorite chair and begin to read. You first turn to the middle of the book. Suddenly you are confronted with names, locations, and actions that make no sense whatsoever. Who in the world are "Bill" or "Joan" or "Judge Mills"? And what are they doing in the Caribbean? And why does Bill suddenly dump one million dollars over the edge of his boat? Confused, you decide to turn to the end of the book to discover the answers. "Joan" and "Judge Mills" are at Bill's funeral.

"You know, Joan, Bill should not have dumped that money over the side of his boat," the judge reflected.

"I know, Judge. But how did Bill know that the Mafia had been following him?" Joan inquired.

Now you are more confused than ever, so you put the book down in disgust. "Grisham has obviously lost his touch. Why can't he write a more coherent book?" you complain to your friend.

I realize that this absurd scenario is about as subtle as a sledge-hammer, and yet it illustrates why so many people have difficulty understanding the subject of Bible prophecy: they start reading the Book in the wrong place. If you want to make sense out of the Bible, the place to start is not in the last book of the Bible (Revelation) or in the middle of the book (Daniel or Ezekiel) but at the beginning of the book. In fact, the name of the first book of the Bible can be translated "beginnings." We call it *Genesis*, and it is the foundation for understanding Bible prophecy.

TRACING OUR SPIRITUAL ROOTS

Whenever we think of the book of Genesis, we think of the land-mark events that marked the beginning of civilization: Creation, the Fall, the first murder, the Flood, and the Tower of Babel. And yet, amazingly, these momentous events are compressed into just eleven chapters of Genesis. It is as if God were saying, "By the way, this is how the world got into the mess it is in now." And that is the theme of Genesis 1–11: man's alienation from God. In these opening chap-ters of Genesis you see man moving further and further away from God until his ultimate act of rebellion at the Tower of Babel.

But beginning in Genesis 12, and extending through the book of Revelation, we see God's reconciliation with man. Although God would have been completely justified in destroying the world after the fiasco at Babel, He announced a plan that would result in salvation instead of condemnation, to those who are willing to believe. At the center of God's rescue plan for humanity is a man named Abraham. And the remaining thirty-nine chapters of Genesis focus on this one man and his family. Why is there so much attention given to Abraham and his family? Because understanding God's promise to Abraham is the key to understanding the rest of the Bible and the end times.

An Unlikely Hero

In the concluding verses of Genesis 11 we find Abraham and his family living in the city of Ur of the Chaldeans (Genesis 11:27–28). Ur was a major commercial city in Mesopotamia. It was comparable in stature to New York or London today. When I was in college, I remember traveling to the University of Texas to view an exhibition of some of the amazing artifacts discovered at Ur, revealing that its citizens were proficient in mathematics, astronomy, and engraving. But the archaeologist's spade has also unearthed the fact that the residents of Ur were idol worshippers.

While we would like to think that Abraham was different from the pagans with whom he lived, Scripture tells us differently. Joshua 24:2–3 clearly shows that Abraham was also an idolater when the Lord appeared to him:

> Joshua said to all the people, "Thus says the LORD, the God of Israel, 'From ancient times your fathers lived beyond

the River, namely, Terah, the father of Abraham and the father of Nahor, and *they* [emphasis mine] served other gods. Then I took your father Abraham from beyond the River, and led him through all the land of Canaan, and multiplied his descendants and gave him Isaac.'"

Allow me to stop for a moment and remind you of the wonderful truth concerning God's grace. If you are a Christian, your coming to Christ had absolutely *nothing* to do with your goodness, but it had everything to do with *God's* goodness. Titus 3:5 tells us that "[God] saved us, not on the basis of deeds which we have done in righteousness, but according to His mercy." God's choice of Abraham was not based on his righteousness—he was just as wicked as any resident of Ur—but on God's undeserved grace.

Thus, God appears to this idol worshipper Abraham and issues this command:

"Go forth from your country, and from your relatives and from your father's house, to the land which I will show you" (Genesis 12:1).

God was telling Abraham that he was supposed to leave everything familiar to him—his country, his friends, his family—to travel to an unknown destination.

We had dinner recently with a new family in our church who could have identified with Abraham. Two years ago they were living in their native country of Mexico. Both the husband and wife had fabulous jobs, they had just completed construction on a beautiful home, and they had recently learned they were going to have a child. *Life doesn't get much better than this,* they thought.

Yet, God had a different plan in mind. A series of sudden difficulties at work convinced this couple that God was leading them to come to the United States, even though neither one of them spoke a word of English. But they knew God had spoken. So they quit their jobs, abandoned their spacious new home, and traveled to this country with nothing more than what they could carry in their suitcases. That takes faith!

It is that same kind of faith that God was asking Abraham to exercise. And yet, with the command came a wonderful promise. In Abraham's case, God followed his command to Abraham with a clear promise:

> Go . . . to the land which I will show you;
> And I will make you a great nation,
> And I will bless you,
> And make your name great;
> And so you shall be a blessing;
> And I will bless those you bless you,
> And the one who curses you I will curse.
> And in you all the families of the earth will be blessed.
> (Genesis 12:1–3)

A THREEFOLD PROMISE

Let's take a moment to examine closely the three elements of this promise that God made to Abraham, which theologians call the *Abrahamic Covenant.*

1. God promised a land.

"Go forth from your country . . . to the *land* which I will show you" (12:1; emphasis mine). God promised to Abraham and his descendants a piece of real estate that would belong to them forever. Later, in Genesis 15:18–21 and Ezekiel 47:13–21 God gave the specific boundaries of the land that would belong to Israel.

Based on these Old Testament descriptions, it is evident that the modern nation of Israel possesses only a fraction of the land area God promised to Abraham's descendants. The greatest amount of this Promised Land that Israel has ever occupied occurred during the reign of Israel's third king, Solomon, from 971 to 931 BC. The basis for the conflict in the Middle East today is Israel's conviction that all of this land belongs to them because of God's promise to Abraham.

2. God promised a seed.

"And I will make you a great nation and I will bless you" (Genesis 12:2). God also promised Abraham that he would be the father of a great nation whose descendants would be as innumerable as the stars in the sky or the sand on the seashore (Genesis 22:17). This is a particularly amazing prophecy considering the fact that Abraham was seventy-five years of age (Hebrews 11:12 describes him as being "as good as dead") and was married to a barren wife (Genesis 11:30).

3. God promised a blessing.

"And in you all the families of the earth will be blessed" (Genesis 12:3). This promise is the obvious climax of God's covenant with Abraham. What did God mean that the entire world would be blessed through Abraham? Some say the fact that Christians, Muslims, and Jews claim Abraham as their spiritual father is a fulfillment of this prophecy. Abraham certainly has been a spiritual blessing to much of the religious world.

But the blessing God has in mind here is much more specific. God was promising that one of Abraham's descendants would be the Savior of the world who would forever remove the curse of sin and death. This promise was a clear prediction of the coming of Christ.

I will admit that in the past I have had difficulty seeing Jesus Christ in this promise. The theological tradition in which I was trained claimed that Abraham would not and could not have had a clear understanding of the coming of Messiah. Abraham trusted God for a land, a seed, and some general blessing, not for a specific Savior. So what changed my mind? Reading the Bible! In Galatians 3, Paul claims that Abraham clearly understood that the blessing mentioned in Genesis 12:3 was directly tied to the coming of Christ.

Before we look at Galatians 3, a little background information might be helpful. Paul wrote this letter to refute the teaching of a group known as the Judaizers who had infected the churches of Galatia. The Judaizers, like so many religious groups today, were teaching that faith in Christ is necessary, but not sufficient, to save a person. "A person must trust in Christ *and* keep the law to be saved," they claimed. Paul is reminding the Galatians that it is faith in Christ alone that saves us. To demonstrate that truth Paul points to Abraham. Abraham? Didn't he live thousands of years before Christ? Yes, but he was still saved by trusting in a God who would exchange Abraham's sin for His righteousness.

> Even so Abraham believed God, and it was reckoned to him as righteousness. Therefore, be sure that it is those who are of faith who are sons of Abraham. The Scripture, foreseeing that God would justify the Gentiles by faith, preached the gospel beforehand to Abraham, saying, "All the nations will be blessed in you." (Galatians 3:6–8)

Do you see it? God promised Abraham that a Savior was coming. And it was Abraham's faith in that promise that caused God to "reckon" righteousness to Abraham. Here in Texas we use the term "reckon" in a different sense ("I reckon it's time to go"). But the Greek word translated "reckon" is an accounting term that means "to put to one's account." If you give me a check for $100, and I deposit it into my bank account, the teller performs an accounting transaction whereby your $100 becomes *my* $100. When Abraham believed in the promise of a Savior, God exchanged Abraham's faith for His righteousness and deposited that righteousness into Abraham's spiritual bank account. From that point on, God viewed Abraham as "not guilty" because of his faith in God's provision for his sin.

Perhaps this illustration will help you understand this concept of "reckoning." Suppose you want to purchase a home. However, like most of us, you need a loan from the bank for a mortgage. Before the loan officer will give you the loan, he wants to see your financial statement revealing how much money you have in the bank, a list of your other assets, and a list of your debts. Unfortunately, your financial statement looks horrible: you recently lost your job, you are swimming in debt, and only have $2 in your checking account! No banker in his right mind would loan you money based on your financial statement. (I reckon you're out of luck!)

That's the bad news. But the good news is that Bill Gates is your father, and his financial statement is in great shape! Out of generosity Dad says to you, "If you would like, I will assume responsibility for your debt. The bank can look to me for the payment. Instead of submitting your financial statement, you can submit mine."

How would you respond to such an offer? If you were filled with pride and stupidity, you might say, "Forget it, Dad. I don't need your help. I can do it on my own. I'll just take my chances with the bank and see if I can't qualify for the loan." And guess what would happen? The bank would look at your financial statement and say, "No deal."

However, you could say, "Dad, I need your help. I've made some bad decisions, I'm practically bankrupt, but I really need that home. I will accept your gracious offer and allow you to take responsibility for this loan." And so, instead of submitting your pitiful financial statement for consideration, you present your dad's. Your application for a new home is not based on your resources, but on his. And Dad's billions are more than sufficient to secure the needed loan.

Now that simple scenario illustrates the most profound truth in the universe. God's universal laws demand that if you are going to secure a home in heaven you must be absolutely perfect. Your righteousness must be equal to that of Jesus Christ. You must obey God's laws perfectly. The problem is that all of us are morally and spiritually bankrupt. We don't have enough righteousness in our spiritual bank account to qualify for heaven. You may have more righteousness in your account than I do; I may have more in my account than Osama Bin Laden had in his; but, none of us has enough. As the Bible says, "For all have sinned and fall short of the glory of God" (Romans 3:23).

Fortunately, we have a generous Father who has made us a great offer. "If you would like," God says, "I will consider your application for heaven, not based on your righteousness, but according to the righteousness of My Son Jesus Christ." And when we trust in Christ's sacrificial death for our sins, God credits or "reckons" our spiritual bank account with the righteousness of Jesus Christ.

Galatians 3 explains that Abraham was saved the same way any of us are saved: by faith. Abraham looked forward to the promised Messiah; we look back at Him. But it is faith in God's provision for our sin that causes God to credit righteousness to our account.

CHARACTERISTICS OF GOD'S PROMISE TO ABRAHAM

We have seen that God's promise to Abraham included the promise of a land, a nation, and a spiritual blessing. An essential key to making sense out of Bible prophecy is to understand three characteristics of God's covenant with Abraham.

1. God's promise to Abraham was literal.

As we saw in the previous section, there was certainly a spiritual component in God's promise to Abraham. But that spiritual blessing does not negate the material nature of the covenant. When God promised to give Abraham and his descendants a land that would be their own, Abraham understood that promise to be a *literal* promise that involved real estate, not a metaphor for heaven. How do I know that? Again, by reading the Bible. Notice how Abraham responded after God's original promise of a land:

> So Abram went forth as the LORD had spoken to him; and Lot went with him. Now Abram was seventy-five years old when he departed from Haran. Abram took Sarai his wife and Lot his nephew, and all their possessions which they had accumulated . . . thus they came to the land of Canaan. (Genesis 12:4–5)

Abraham's immediate reaction to God's promise was to pack up and head out to that new land! Remember, there was no *Mayflower* or Bekins back then to assist them in their relocation. Can you imagine how much stuff Abraham must have accumulated in his seventy-five years of life? We have only been in our present home for six years and our two-car garage doesn't have room for one car (or even a bicycle). I can't fathom what it will look like after seventy-five years. Why would Abraham and Sarai endure the headache of such a mammoth move if the "land" God promised was a reference to some celestial city in the afterlife?

Make no mistake about it, Abraham was looking forward to a heavenly home. The writer of Hebrews records that Abraham was "looking for the city which has foundations, whose architect and builder is God" (11:10). But Abraham's heavenly focus did not conflict with his earthly pursuit. Abraham took God's promise at face value and acted accordingly by moving to that promised land.

2. God's promise to Abraham was eternal.

God's promise to Abraham and his descendants of a land, a nation, and a blessing was not limited by time. On several occasions when Abraham was plagued by doubt or discouragement, God repeated His original promise to Abraham. One of those times was in Genesis 13 after a conflict that had separated Abraham from his nephew Lot.

> The LORD said to Abram, after Lot had separated from him, "Now lift up your eyes and look from the place where you are, northward and southward and eastward and westward; for all the land which you see, I will give it to you and to your descendants *forever.*" (Genesis 13:14–15; emphasis mine)

We mere mortals have a difficult time with the concept of "forever." How long is eternity? Henry Willen Van Loon writes, "High up in the north, in the land called Svithjod, there stands a rock. It is 100 miles high and 100 miles wide. Once every 1,000 years a little bird comes to this rock to sharpen its beak. When the rock has thus been worn away, then a single day of eternity will have gone by."[1] Obviously, the term "forever" in the above verse guarantees that God's promise to Abraham and his descendants would endure for a long time!

3. God's promise to Abraham was unconditional.

This is the most important characteristic of God's promise to Abraham for our understanding of prophecy. Many Christians will concede that God's promise to Abraham was a literal promise in its original form. However, because of Israel's subsequent disobedience and disbelief, some believe that God revoked His promise to Abraham and made the Church the beneficiary of the covenant. Furthermore, these promises originally made to Israel have been transformed into spiritual blessings for the Church: the land promised to Israel is now heaven for the Church; the throne from which Messiah will rule is no longer located in Jerusalem but in heaven (or in Christians' hearts); the promised reign of Christ upon the earth is being fulfilled right now instead of in a future Millennium (a one-thousand year period of time we will discuss in subsequent chapters).

Now, I will admit that such reasoning *sounds* logical . . . and even biblical. God made numerous conditional promises to the

Israelites. For example, consider Moses' words to the Israelites before they entered into the Promised Land:

> See, I am setting before you today a blessing and a curse:
> the blessing, if you listen to the commandments of the
> LORD your God, which I am commanding you today; and
> the curse, if you do not listen to the commandments of
> the LORD your God, but turn aside from the way which I
> am commanding you today, by following other gods which
> you have not known. (Deuteronomy 11:26–28)

Since that time, Israel's history has been filled with blessings and curses. Obedience has resulted in peace and prosperity; disobedience has resulted in calamity and exile. Yet, such warnings do not negate the unconditional nature of God's promise to Abraham and his descendants.

For example, shortly after my oldest daughter was born and even before our second daughter was born, Amy and I prepared our wills which leave everything to our children. At the time we drew up our wills we did not know what our children would be like or even how many children we would have; nevertheless, everything would be equally divided among our offspring upon our deaths.

As our daughters matured, we established rules around our house; our own list of "blessings and curses" à la Deuteronomy. "If you perform your chores, you get your allowance; if you mouth off to your parents, you forfeit your allowance." While they were living under our roof, our girls experienced both blessings and curses under our system of rules. But although their disobedience occasionally caused them to lose their allowance and experience our wrath, it never endangered their ultimate inheritance. They are our children, and no amount of disobedience will cause them to forfeit their birthright.

In the same way, disobedience to God's law (which came to Moses four hundred years *after* God's promise to Abraham) brought God's severe discipline, but it never endangered the inheritance of the believing Israelites. The apostle Paul explains it this way:

> What I am saying is this: the Law, which came four hundred and thirty years later, does not invalidate a covenant previously ratified by God, so as to nullify the promise. For if the inheritance is based on law, it is no longer based on a promise; but God has granted it to Abraham by means of a promise. (Galatians 3:17–18)

The psalmist also understood the difference between God's conditional and unconditional promises to Israel:

> If his sons forsake My law
> And do not walk in My judgments,
> If they violate My statutes
> And do not keep My commandments,
> Then I will punish their transgression with the rod
> And their iniquity with stripes.
> But I will not break off My lovingkindness from him,

Nor deal falsely in My faithfulness.

My covenant I will not violate,

Nor will I alter the utterance of My lips.

(Psalm 89:30–34)

Perhaps the greatest evidence for the unconditional nature of the Abrahamic Covenant is in the ratification of that covenant as recorded in Genesis 15. Abraham understandably wanted assurance that God would do what He had promised to do. So he asks,

"O Lord God, how may I know that I will possess it?" So He said to him, "Bring Me a three year old heifer, and a three year old female goat, and a three year old ram, and a turtle dove, and a young pigeon." Then he brought all these to Him and cut them in two, and laid each half opposite the other; but he did not cut the birds. (Genesis 15:8–10)

In Abraham's day, whenever two leaders made an agreement with one another, they would cut the animals into two parts along the backbone and place them in two rows, facing each other with a space in between them. Then the two parties making the covenant would walk together between the animal pieces, signifying the responsibility each party had to keep his part of the agreement. Using this familiar ritual, God ordered Abraham to cut the animals into two pieces, leaving a path between the animals. But then God does something most unusual. Instead of walking with Abraham between the pieces of the animal, God put Abraham to sleep!

Now when the sun was going down, a deep sleep fell upon Abram; and behold, terror and great darkness fell upon him (Genesis 15:12).

God, represented by a smoking oven and a flaming torch, walked through the animal pieces by *Himself*:

It came about when the sun had set, that it was very dark, and behold, there appeared a smoking oven and a flaming torch which passed between these pieces. On that day the LORD made a covenant with Abram. (Genesis 15:17–18)

God was demonstrating to Abraham, and to all subsequent generations, that His promise to Abraham was unconditional. This agreement did not depend upon Abraham and his descendants keeping their end of the bargain. The fulfillment of this promise rested solely on the faithfulness of God. And that is why Hebrews 6:13 says, "For when God made the promise to Abraham, since He could swear by no one greater, He swore by Himself."

THE PROMISE TODAY

What does the promise made to Abraham have to do with our understanding of Bible prophecy? God *is* going to fulfill the promise that He made to Abraham and his believing descendants. Since 1948 Israel has been occupying a portion of the land God has promised, but it has never possessed *all* of the land promised to Abraham in Genesis 15:18–21 and Ezekiel 47:13–21. Although a descendant of Abraham's (Jesus Christ) did come to bring a spiritual blessing to the entire world, the Messiah is not yet ruling over the entire earth as God later promised to David, Isaiah, and the prophets.

To put it bluntly, God has some unfinished business here on planet earth. And the rest of the Bible, from Genesis 12 to Revelation 22, is the story of God's ultimate fulfillment of His promises to Abraham and his spiritual descendants.

You may wonder why you should be concerned about God keeping His promise to Israel. What difference does it make to those of us who are not Israelites? The same God who has made unconditional promises to believing Israel has also made unconditional promises to you and to me.

> And I give eternal life to them, and they will never perish; and no one will snatch them out of my hand. (John 10:28) Therefore He is able also to save forever those who draw near to God through him, since He always lives to make intercession for them. (Hebrews 7:25)

> For He Himself has said, "I will never desert you, nor will I ever forsake you." (Hebrews 13:5)

How can we know that God will not change His mind and rescind those promises He has made to us about eternal life? How can we be sure that when we stand before God, He will not say, "I know you were depending on Christ to save you, but I have changed my mind. I am going to judge you by your works instead of grace"? Our only hope is that God is a God of integrity who will keep His word. Fortunately for us, Romans 11:29 promises that "the gifts and the calling of God are irrevocable."

The same God who can be trusted to fulfill His pledge to you will also keep His covenant with Abraham—a covenant that not only affects Israel, but the entire world . . . as we will discover in the following chapters.

III

GETTING THE BIG PICTURE

Maps can be useful in navigating through unfamiliar terri-tory. Unfortunately, I had to learn the value of maps the hard way some years ago. A pastor friend had invited me to Canada to speak at his church's annual Valentine banquet. I departed the Dallas–Ft. Worth airport early one morning and, after a plane change in Minneapolis, landed in Winnipeg around 4:00 that after-noon with plenty of time to spare. After retrieving my luggage, I stood out front waiting . . . waiting . . . and waiting for my host to arrive. After about thirty minutes, I strolled back inside the terminal to call the pastor's home. When I looked at the information letter he had mailed a few weeks earlier, I noticed that the city and prov-ince on the letterhead did not correspond to my present location. Because I had preached for the pastor at his church in Winnipeg ten years earlier, I had assumed he was still in the same location.

I took the letter to the airline counter, explaining that I had apparently traveled to the wrong city. According to the letter, I needed to be in Vancouver, British Columbia. Not knowing much about Canada, I innocently asked, "Is there a bus I can catch to Vancouver? I need to be there in about thirty minutes."

"A *bus*?!" All the employees behind the counter exclaimed in unison. "You've got to be kidding! Vancouver is fifteen hundred miles from here!"

Fortunately, a plane was getting ready to depart for Vancouver in the next few minutes. Even though it was a three-hour flight, the two-hour time change worked to my advantage, and I arrived at the church just in time to preach. As I was boarding the flight that evening, the ticket agent handed me a map of Canada (apparently the story of my mistake had already traveled from the ticket counter to the departure gate). "Here, read this; it might help you next time!" she chuckled. Since then, I have been a firm believer in maps—especially when traveling in a foreign country!

To most people, Bible prophecy is such a country. Although many of us have a vague understanding of end-time events (things are supposed to get worse, Jesus is coming back, and Christians will live happily ever after), we would find it difficult to define the major events of Bible prophecy and place them in sequential order. Let's take a moment and test *your* knowledge of end-time events.

See if you can write a one-sentence description of each of the following events as if you were trying to explain it to a friend who had little knowledge of the Bible. (If you find that too easy, then also give a supporting Scripture reference that describes each of these events):

- The Great White Throne Judgment
- The Tribulation
- The Rapture
- The Millennium
- The Church Age

And now for the bonus round, explain the differences between:

- Premillennialism
- Amillennialism
- Postmillennialism
- Pretribulation Rapture
- Midtribulation Rapture
- Posttribulation Rapture

Not only would the majority of Christians find it impossible to complete the above quiz, they would wax eloquently about why such details are unimportant: "I'm not on the planning committee for Christ's return; I'm on the welcoming committee." "I don't want to be so heavenly-minded that I'm no earthly good."

Yet, as we have already seen, a basic understanding of end-time events is both important *and* possible. In this chapter we are going to briefly define each of the major end-time events, along with the major supporting scriptures for each event, according to the Premillennial, Pretribulation Rapture view (don't worry, we'll get to all of that later). We will conclude the chapter by briefly looking at how Jesus tied all of these events together in Matthew 24–25.

The following chart shows in sequence the major prophetic events that are yet to occur.

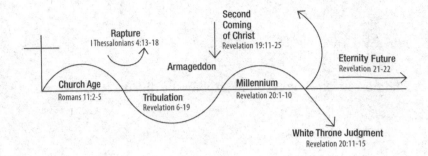

1. The Church Age (Romans 11:25)

Imagine the following situation. You want to give your ten-year-old son a birthday party he will never forget. You purchase an exquisite cake, hire an expensive entertainer, and send out elaborate invitations to your extended family several weeks ahead of time. However, the day before your son's party every one of your family members calls and sends his regrets. They offer all kinds of flimsy excuses why they cannot attend the gathering. Not wanting to disappoint your son, you quickly begin calling friends, acquaintances, and neighbors and inviting them to attend the party.

Jesus used the above illustration (more or less) to explain the time we are living in now, known as "The Church Age" (see Matthew 22:2–14). The Church Age is that period of time from Pentecost until the Rapture (a term we will discuss in the next section) during which Gentiles are invited to participate in the blessings of the Abrahamic Covenant. In the Church Age, God has extended the "invitation list" to be part of God's kingdom beyond the Jews to include anyone who will accept His offer of salvation.

Since the time of Genesis 12, the story of the Bible is the story of God's dealings with the nation of Israel. Over a period of thousands of years, God has attempted to bring Israel into a right relationship with Himself. Although there are many instances in the Old Testament of non-Jews (Gentiles) being saved, the primary focus has been on Israel. However, after Israel rejected Jesus Christ, God temporarily halted His dealings with Israel and turned His attention toward the Gentiles. The key word here is "temporarily." In Romans 11, Paul explains that God is not through with Israel. Her hardness of heart is only a temporary condition:

> I say then, God has not rejected His people, has He? May it never be! For I too am an Israelite, a descendant of Abraham, of the tribe of Benjamin. . . . For I do not want you, brethren, to be uninformed of this mystery—so that you will not be wise in your own estimation—that a partial hardening has happened to Israel until the fullness of the Gentiles has come in. (Romans 11:1, 25)

Because Israel rejected Christ, we who are Gentiles got invited to the party! Yet, God has not permanently turned His back on Israel. As we saw in the last chapter, God will one day fulfill His promise to believing Israel of a land, a seed, and a blessing. God has one final event in mind to turn the Israelites toward Himself: the

Great Tribulation. But before that final period of dealing with Israel can begin, another event must first occur.

2. The Rapture of the Church (1 Thessalonians 4:13–18)

As you can see on the chart, the Church Age will end with an event many refer to as the "Rapture of the Church." The word *rapture* comes from a Greek word *harpazo*, which means "to snatch away." That is what the Rapture is—a snatching away of all believers before the beginning of the Tribulation. The signal passage in the New Testament that describes the Rapture is 1 Thessalonians 4:16–18:

> For the Lord Himself will descend from heaven with a shout, with the voice of the archangel and with the trumpet of God, and the dead in Christ will rise first. Then we who are alive and remain will be caught up together with them in the clouds to meet the Lord in the air, and so we shall always be with the Lord. Therefore comfort one another with these words.

There are three different views regarding the timing of the Rapture. Those who believe in a Pretribulation Rapture teach that the Rapture will occur before the Great Tribulation; those who advocate a Posttribulation Rapture believe that the Rapture will occur at the end of the Tribulation and will be almost concurrent with the Second Coming of Christ; and still others believe in a

Midtribulation Rapture that will occur after the first three and one-half years of the Tribulation. We will discuss the pros and cons of each viewpoint in the next chapter.

A number of fine evangelical scholars dismiss the whole idea of a Rapture by raising a number of questions:

- If the Rapture is a reality, why is the term not found in the Bible?
- Why did Jesus fail to mention the Rapture of the Church?
- Doesn't a Rapture assume there are three comings of Christ instead of two?
- How can anyone believe that the Church will escape the suffering of the Tribulation, given the long history of suffering by God's people?

We will examine each of these objections in the next chapter.

3. The Tribulation (Revelation 6–19)

Following the Rapture of the Church is a time commonly referred to as "The Tribulation," a seven-year period that begins when the world dictator, known as Antichrist, signs a peace covenant with Israel and ends with Armageddon and the Second Coming of Jesus Christ. The purpose of the Tribulation is twofold: (1) the redemption of Israel, and (2) the condemnation of unbelievers. As we will see in chapter 5, the Old Testament prophets wrote extensively about this future time in Israel's history, referring to it as "the day

of the Lord" or the time of "Jacob's trouble." God will severely discipline unbelieving Israel during these years through the Antichrist.

The purpose of God's discipline, however, will be redemptive as
evidenced by the conversion of 144,000 Jews at the beginning of
the Tribulation. These Jewish converts will serve as missionaries
throughout the world during the Tribulation. Although many Jews
and Gentiles will be saved through their witness, these converts
will pay a heavy price for their conversion. The Tribulation will
also be a time for God to pour out His wrath on unbelievers. Three
series of judgments (seals, trumpets, and bowls) will result in the
deaths of millions and the destruction of a large part of the planet.

If the purposes of the Tribulation are the discipline of Israel and
the judgment of unbelievers, what about the Church? What happens to Christians prior to the beginning of the Tribulation? One of
the strongest arguments for the Pretribulation Rapture (a snatching
away of the Church before the Tribulation) is that the Tribulation is
designed for Israel and unbelievers instead of the Church. We will
explore this truth more in the next chapter.

4. The Second Coming of Christ (Revelation 19:11–16)

The climax of the Tribulation will occur during the war of
Armageddon, during which the major powers of the world will
seek to defeat Antichrist and his forces. However, as the world
forces prepare to destroy one another, the heavens will suddenly
open and all attention will be directed upward as the entire world
sees a sight they will never forget:

And I saw heaven opened, and behold, a white horse, and He who sat on it is called Faithful and True, and in righteousness He judges and wages war. . . . And the armies which are in heaven, clothed in fine linen, white and clean, were following Him on white horses. From His mouth comes a sharp sword, so that with it He may strike down the nations, and He will rule them with a rod of iron; and He treads the wine press of the fierce wrath of God, the Almighty. And on His robe and on His thigh He has a name written, "King of kings and Lord of lords." (Revelation 19:11, 14–16)

This passage describes the "Second Coming of Christ," which is the *visible* return of Jesus Christ to establish His kingdom on earth. Although there are some similarities between the Rapture and the Second Coming, they are two entirely different events. At the Rapture, the Lord comes secretly for His children. He appears in the clouds only to His followers, and His feet never touch the earth. However, at the Second Coming, believers and unbelievers alike will witness Christ's return to the earth.

5. The Millennium (Revelation 20:1–3)

"The Millennium" is the thousand-year period of time during which Christ will reign on the earth, fulfilling God's promises to Abraham and his believing descendants. As we saw in the last chapter, God made a literal, eternal, and unconditional promise to Abraham that his descendants would one day possess a specific land and that one of his descendants would rule the entire world. The Old Testament prophets anxiously anticipated this earthly reign of Messiah. For example, consider these familiar words of Isaiah:

> But with righteousness He will judge the poor...
> And with the breath of His lips He will slay the wicked....
> And the wolf will dwell with the lamb,
> And the leopard will lie down with the young goat....
> They will not hurt or destroy in all My holy mountain,
> For the earth will be full of the knowledge of the LORD
> As the waters cover the sea. (Isaiah 11:4, 6, 9)

As we will see in chapter 7, it is impossible to place these extensive Old Testament prophecies about Christ's rule on the earth in this present age or in eternity. There must be a future time, prior to the new heaven and earth described in Revelation 21–22, when God will fulfill these promises to believing Israel. That time will be the Millennium.

6. The Great White Throne Judgment (Revelation 20:11–15)

Although only Christians will enter into the Millennium (those unbelievers who survive the Tribulation will be judged at the Second Coming of Christ), there will be people born during the Millennium who will choose to follow Satan rather than Christ. (Chapter 8 will explain both how people will be born in the

Millennium and how some of those people will be deceived by Satan.) Nevertheless, the Bible teaches that both of these realities will precipitate God's final judgment of all unbelievers at an event known as the "Great White Throne Judgment."

Revelation 20 describes this judgment in detail:

> Then I saw a great white throne and Him who sat upon it, from whose presence earth and heaven fled away, and no place was found for them. And I saw the dead, the great and the small, standing before the throne, and the books were opened; and another book was opened, which is the book of life; and the dead were judged from the things which were written in the books, according to their deeds. And the sea gave up the dead which were in it, and death and Hades gave up the dead which were in them; and they were judged every one of them according to their deeds. . . . And if anyone's name was not found written in the book of life, he was thrown into the lake of fire. (Revelation 20:11–13, 15)

Although we will explain this judgment in much greater detail in chapter 8, notice several important characteristics of this judgment. First, the *subjects* of the judgments are unbelievers. The occupants of Hades (the temporary dwelling place of unbelievers who die) are the ones who stand before the Great White Throne (Revelation 20:11).

The *basis* for their judgments is their works (Revelation 20:12–13). Since these unbelievers have refused the grace of Jesus Christ, they will be judged as they have chosen to be judged, according to their works.

Finally, the *result* of the judgment will be eternal damnation (Revelation 20:15). Unbelievers are not simply destroyed, but they are sentenced to an eternity of suffering.

7. Eternity Future (Revelation 21–22)

After the Great White Throne Judgment, the present earth will be completely destroyed by fire. The apostle Peter wrote of that event in his second letter:

> But by His word the present heavens and earth are being reserved for fire, kept for the day of judgment and destruction of ungodly men. . . . But the day of the Lord will come like a thief, in which the heavens will pass away with a roar and the elements will be destroyed with intense heat, and the earth and its works will be burned up. (2 Peter 3:7, 10)

Following the destruction of this present earth will be the unveiling of a new heaven and earth, as witnessed by the apostle John:

> Then I saw a new heaven and a new earth; for the first heaven and the first earth passed away, and there is no longer any sea. And I saw the holy city, new Jerusalem, coming down out of heaven from God, made ready as a bride adorned for her husband. And I heard a loud voice

from the throne, saying, "Behold, the tabernacle of God is among men, and He will dwell among them, and they shall be His people, and God Himself will be among them, and He will wipe away every tear from their eyes; and there will no longer be any death; there will no longer be any mourning, or crying, or pain; the first things have passed away. (Revelation 21:1–4)

It is significant that John saw both a new heaven *and* a new earth. Many Christians have been taught that our eternal home will be in heaven. But as we will see in chapter 10, *earth*, not heaven, will be our final destination. I don't know about you, but I get excited about that truth since floating around on a cloud for eternity has never had much appeal to me!

IT IS OUR BUSINESS

Do we really need to know about all of these events? Last year as I stood on the Mount of Olives near Jerusalem, I thought about the question the disciples had asked Jesus in that exact location two thousand years earlier: "Tell us, when will these things happen, and what will be the sign of Your coming, and of the end of the age?" (Matthew 24:3). Unlike some today who dismiss Bible prophecy as an irrelevant and unintelligible subject, Jesus said it's important to understand end-time events (notice that He devoted two chapters to His answer), and He clearly explained those events. First, He described the Tribulation:

For nation will rise against nation, and kingdom against kingdom, and in various places there will be famines and earthquakes. . . . "Therefore when you see the abomination of desolation which was spoken of through Daniel the prophet, standing in the holy place (let the reader understand), then those who are in Judea must flee to the mountains." (Matthew 24:7, 15–16)

Jesus said the Tribulation would be followed by His return to earth:

But immediately after the tribulation of those days the sun will be darkened, and the moon will not give its light, and the stars will fall from the sky, and the powers of the heavens will be shaken. And then the sign of the Son of Man will appear in the sky, and then all the tribes of the earth will mourn, and they will see the Son of Man coming on the clouds of the sky with power and great glory. (Matthew 24:29–30)

Then, Jesus described His judgment of unbelievers:

But when the Son of Man comes in His glory, and all the angels with Him, then He will sit on His glorious throne. All the nations will be gathered before Him; and He will separate them from one another, as the shepherd separates the sheep from the goats . . . Then the King will say to those on His right, "Come, you who are blessed of My Father, inherit the kingdom prepared for you from the foundation of the world." . . . Then He will also say to those on His left, "Depart from Me, accursed ones, into the eternal fire which has been prepared for the devil and his angels." (Matthew 25:31–32, 34, 41)

Although Jesus said His disciples could not know the date of His return (Matthew 24:36), He never rebuked them for wanting to understand the events surrounding His return. An understanding of Bible prophecy is both important *and* possible, as Matthew 24–25 demonstrates.

But Matthew 24–25 also raises a question. According to Jesus' reply, the next significant prophetic event would be the Tribulation. Why did Jesus fail to mention the Rapture of the Church? Are Christians going to have to endure this time of unparalleled punishment? Before you build a bomb shelter in your backyard and load up on cans of tuna fish and peanut butter, you might want to read the next chapter.

Chapter Four

||||||||||||||||||||||||||||||||||||||||||

NOT LEFT BEHIND

A discussion of end-time events produces various reactions among different people. When I was a student in high school, our English teacher instructed us to present "as creatively as possible" a report on the book of our choice. I chose Hal Lindsey's best-selling prophecy book *The Late Great Planet Earth*, reasoning that my report would be a great witnessing opportunity, especially since our teacher was Jewish. I spent the first thirty minutes of the presentation explaining the events that will precede the Second Coming of Christ, giving particular emphasis to the invasion of Israel by forces from the north that Lindsey identified as Russia. This was particularly interesting to our class since then President Nixon was in Moscow trying to ease tensions with the Soviet Union. What no one in the class knew was that I had prearranged for our assistant principal to interrupt my presentation by coming over the intercom at a designated time with this announcement: "Students and faculty. We have just received word from United Press International that Russia has invaded Israel.

President Nixon is returning from Moscow to Washington at this hour. Students and faculty are urged to leave immediately and seek shelter."

My teacher shouted, "Oh, my God! It's true! It's true!" as she and the students headed for the exit. I quickly assured them that it was just part of the presentation, intended to demonstrate how current world events coincided with biblical prophecy. Unfortunately, the assistant principal made a mistake. Instead of piping the announcement into our room only, he flipped the wrong switch and the entire school heard the evacuation command, without benefit of my explanation. Suddenly I heard lockers slamming and people shouting as three thousand people started filing out of the school! Forty years later some of my classmates still remind me of that spring day when it looked as if the world might end. At least I made my point—though my grade on the project did not reflect appropriate appreciation from my teacher (who remained unconvinced and unconverted).

The events that immediately precede the Second Coming of Christ will indeed be terrifying to unbelievers: wars, earthquakes, famine, and economic chaos. Fortunately, Christians will not experience those hardships because of an event that is the focus of this chapter: the Rapture of the Church. Many people do not accept the idea of a snatching away of the Church prior to the Tribulation, but as we view this event in the context of God's prophetic plan, I think you will understand why a Rapture of the Church is both biblical and essential.

EVERYONE LOVES A MYSTERY

In chapter 2 we explored God's promise to Abraham and his descendants of a land, a seed, and a blessing. We saw that this was a plan that was literal, eternal, and unconditional, meaning that one day God is obligated to fulfill his promise to believing Israel. That is certainly good news for the Jews, but what about the rest of us who are not Jews? How does the Abrahamic Covenant benefit us?

Throughout the Old Testament there were hints— strong hints—that God's blessings would extend to Gentiles also. In the Abrahamic Covenant itself, God promised Abraham that "in you all the families of the earth will be blessed" (Genesis 12:3). Ruth, Rahab, and the residents of Nineveh are just three examples of Gentiles in the Old Testament who were the beneficiaries of God's grace through what was originally promised to Abraham.

In the New Testament, Jesus also alluded to believing Gentiles receiving God's grace. When Jesus told a story about a king who invited people off the street to attend his son's wedding banquet when the invited guests failed to respond, the Pharisees knew exactly what Jesus was teaching: because of Israel's rejection of Christ, God would allow Gentiles to be fellow heirs to the promises of God (Matthew 22:1–14). Such an idea was so distasteful to the Jews that when Jesus finished His story, "the Pharisees went and plotted together how they might trap Him in what He said" (Matthew 22:15).

Yet, in spite of these strong hints, the Old Testament prophets and the apostles did not fully grasp the idea of Gentiles being recipients of God's promises. This was a "mystery" left to the apostle Paul to explain:

> That by revelation there was made known to me the mystery, as I wrote before in brief. . . . which in other generations was not made known to the sons of men, as it has now been revealed to His holy apostles and prophets in the Spirit; to be specific, that the Gentiles are fellow heirs and fellow members of the body, and fellow partakers of the promise in Christ Jesus through the gospel. (Ephesians 3:3, 5–6)

Whenever we read the word "mystery" we think of something eerie, like an old Alfred Hitchcock thriller or the latest Patricia Cornwell novel. But the word translated "mystery" simply refers to something previously hidden that has now been revealed. Paul is saying that God gave him the task to unveil this mystery: that Gentiles would be fellow recipients with the Jews of God's blessings.

What does such a mystery have to do with the Rapture of the Church? It explains why neither the Old Testament nor Jesus ever mentioned it. Remember in the last chapter we saw that when the disciples asked the Lord about the events preceding His return, Jesus began with the Tribulation, not the Rapture. The diagram below detail the events explained by Jesus in Matthew 24–25:

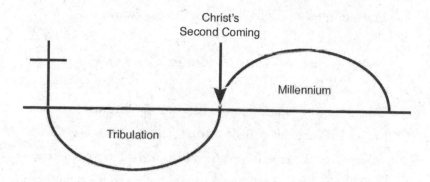

Why is there no mention of a Rapture of the Church by the Old Testament writers or by Jesus? Because the whole idea of a Church Age during which Gentiles would come to faith in Christ was a mystery that the prophets did not fully grasp and Jesus chose not to reveal. Jesus told His Jewish disciples that as far as Israel was concerned, the next event on God's prophetic timetable was a time of tribulation that would end with the return of the Lord and the establishment of His kingdom.

But when Israel rejected Christ, God hit the "stop" button on His prophetic stopwatch. There are seven years remaining on the clock known as the Tribulation during which God will give Israel one last chance to repent. But before those final seven years begin, God is giving Gentiles an opportunity to trust in Christ. This "pause" in God's program is the time we call the Church Age. See Romans 11:25:

For I do not want you, brethren, to be uninformed of this mystery—so that you will not be wise in your own estimation—that a partial hardening has happened to Israel until the fullness of the Gentiles has come in.

Israel's rejection of Christ has caused God to *temporarily* set aside His plans with Israel. However, during this parentheses in God's dealings with Israel, Gentiles have the opportunity to trust in Christ. We have actually benefited from Israel's rejection of Christ! But when all of the Gentiles who will be saved have been saved, God will hit the "start" button of the stopwatch, and the final seven years of God's dealings with Israel will commence.

Whew! I realize that is a lot of content to digest, so let's take a breather while I tell you a sad story from my love life. Don't worry; it has a happy ending. My wife, Amy, and I met in Mrs. Denny's seventh-grade math class when we were twelve years old. It was love at first sight! We started dating in the ninth grade, but when we became sophomores in high school, Amy made what I considered to be a foolish decision: she decided she wanted to date other guys. Her decision broke my heart. To paraphrase the country-western song, "She dun' stomped on my aorta!"

After moping around for several months, I decided to make the most of all the free time I suddenly had. I organized several Bible studies and started spending time with friends who were not yet Christians. One of those friends was a girl in my English class who was very interested in spiritual matters. After several months she prayed to trust in Christ as her Savior. Later that year, Amy and I got back together and have enjoyed a wonderful relationship (despite her "temporary insanity" during our sopho-more year!).

A few years ago, I received a letter from that girl I had led to Christ. She told me all about her spiritual growth and thanked me for the part I played in God's plan. Then she made this observa-tion: "It's funny, but if Amy had not broken up with you that year, I doubt you would have ever taken the time to share Christ with me." That's a great picture of what God has done with the Jews and the Gentiles. Because of Israel's rejection of Christ, the Gentiles have been given an opportunity to believe. But like Amy, Israel's hard-ness of heart (sorry, dear) is only temporary. Once the "fullness of the Gentiles" (the Church Age) is complete, God will resume His final time of dealing with Israel. Yet, before that final seven years commences, the Bible teaches that God is going to remove His Church from the earth in the event known as the Rapture.

THE RAPTURE IN SCRIPTURE

Since Paul is the one to whom God chose to reveal the mystery of the Church Age, it should be no surprise that Paul is also the one who revealed the event that would end the Church Age: the Rapture. First Thessalonians 4–5 is the New Testament passage that most clearly outlines the details of this event. Paul wrote this letter to encourage a group of Christians who were discouraged at the Lord's delayed return. They fully believed that Jesus would return in their lifetimes. Now that some of their loved ones were begin-ning to die, they were filled with questions:

- "What happens to our loved ones who die before the Lord returns? Will they miss out on the resurrection?"
- "What about those of us who are alive when Christ returns? Do we receive our resurrection bodies then or later?"

And so Paul gives this word of explanation:

> But we do not want you to be uniformed, brethren, about those who are asleep, so that you may not grieve as do the rest who have no hope. For if we believe that Jesus died and rose again, even so God will bring with Him those who have fallen asleep in Jesus. (1 Thessalonians 4:13–14)

A word of explanation about the term *asleep* might be helpful here. Paul uses that term to explain what happens to a Christian's body at death, not his spirit (the essence of who we are). The Bible never teaches that a Christian's spirit goes to sleep when he dies. When a believer dies, his or her spirit goes immediately into the presence of Christ. Paul wrote in 2 Corinthians 5:8 that "to be absent from the body" is "to be at home with the Lord." Thus, the term *sleep* refers to the physical body of a Christian. Let's continue.

> For this we say to you by the word of the Lord, that we who are alive and remain until the coming of the Lord, will not precede those who have fallen asleep. For the Lord Himself will descend from heaven with a shout, with the

voice of the archangel and with the trumpet of God, and the dead in Christ will rise first. Then we who are alive and remain will be caught up together with them in the clouds to meet the Lord in the air, and so we shall always be with the Lord. Therefore comfort one another with these words. (1 Thessalonians 4:15–18)

Notice the four ingredients of the Rapture Paul explains in this passage:

1. Christ will descend from heaven.

The first aspect of the Rapture is the descent of Christ from heaven. "The Lord Himself will descend from heaven" (v. 16). At the Rapture the Lord Jesus Christ will appear to His followers, not on earth, but "in the air" (v. 17). In verse 15 Paul describes the Rapture as "the coming of the Lord." The word translated "coming" is the Greek word *parousia* which is also used in Matthew 24:27 to describe the Second Coming of Christ:

For just as the lightning comes from the east and flashes even to the west, so will the *coming* of the Son of Man be. (Matthew 24:27; emphasis mine)

You may be asking, "Robert, doesn't the fact that the same word is used to describe both the Rapture and the Second Coming prove that they are one in the same?" Not at all. My friend and former professor, Dr. Charles Ryrie, makes a significant point when he reminds us that just because things are similar does not mean they are identical.[1] For example, my car has a motor; my washing machine has a motor; and my garage door opener has a motor. But are these three items identical? Of course not.

Similarly, just because the Rapture and the Second Coming of Christ are similar in some respects does not mean they are the same event. Suppose, Dr. Ryrie theorizes, that some proud grandparents say to their friends, "We are looking forward to the coming of our grandchildren next week," and then later in the conversation say, "We are excited that our grandchildren will be coming for our golden wedding anniversary." From those two statements you could assume that (a) the grandparents are saying that their anniversary is next week and, thus, are speaking of their grandchildren's arrival and their anniversary as a single event; or (b) the grandparents are referring to two different events—the grandchildren are coming next week for a visit, but they will also be returning at a later time for the anniversary celebration.

The fact that the Lord is coming at both the Rapture and the Second Coming does not mean that these two events are identical. While there are some similarities between the Rapture and the Second Coming, there are also many differences that we will more fully explore in chapter 6. But one major difference between these events is mentioned in 1 Thessalonians 4:17: "Then we who are alive and remain will be caught up together with them in the clouds to meet the Lord in the air."

At the Rapture, Christ appears "in the air" without setting foot on the earth; at the Second Coming, "His feet will stand on the Mount of Olives, which is in front of Jerusalem on the east" (Zechariah 14:4). Although Christ will appear in the clouds, the Rapture is not so much about His coming as it is our going!

2. The dead in Christ will be resurrected.

The second aspect of the Rapture is the resurrection of the physical bodies of the "dead in Christ." When we die, our spirit goes immediately into the presence of Christ. But our body is left behind, just as the body of Christ remained in the tomb until that first Easter morning. However, our body will not remain in the grave forever. When the trumpet of God sounds, "the dead in Christ will rise first" (I Thessalonians 4:16). The graves will be opened and the bodies of believers will rise toward heaven.

Who are "the dead in Christ" whose bodies will be raised at the Rapture? Some believe they include all believers since the beginning of time—Adam, Eve, Abraham, Moses, David, Ruth, Rahab, and all of the Old Testament saints. However, I believe that the term "dead in Christ" refers only to those believers who have died since the ascension of Christ and the beginning of the Church Age we discussed earlier. The Rapture is an event for the Church.

If that is true, then when do these other believers receive their new bodies? We will discuss that issue in chapter 8. But in this passage, Paul is addressing Christians who have died in the Church Age. He is comforting those Thessalonians who have lost loved ones by saying, "Death is not as final as it seems. Your loved ones have not missed out on the coming of the Lord. In fact, they will be the first to receive their brand new bodies."

As I write these words, tears fill my eyes as I think about a little cemetery in Van Alstyne, Texas, where the bodies of my great-grandmother, my grandmother, my grandfather, my mother, and my father are buried. That plot of ground has been the site of some of the saddest moments of my life as I have repeatedly wept over the loss of those people whom I loved most. But one day, Paul says, that place of defeat will become a place of victory when God has the final word and forever defeats the power of the grave.

3. All living Christians will be removed.

After the resurrection of the "dead in Christ," Paul explains that those Christians who are alive at the time of the Rapture will be suddenly "caught up together with them in the clouds to meet the Lord in the air" (1 Thessalonians 4:16–17). This means that there will be a generation of Christians who will never experience death. Their entire being—body, soul, and spirit—will suddenly be removed from the earth, just as Enoch and Elijah in the Old Testament were transported to heaven without ever experiencing death.

One common objection to the idea of a Rapture is that the term is never used in the Bible. If that were true, it would not negate the reality of the Rapture. For example, we believe in the Trinity (the Father, the Son, and the Holy Spirit) even though the word "Trinity" is never found in the Bible. However, the term *Rapture* is a biblical term. The Latin translation of "caught up" in 1 Thessalonians 4:17 is *rapturo,* from which we derive the English word *rapture.* The original Greek term *harpazo* is used in the New Testament thirteen times and in two instances describes the physical removal of a person from the earth.

For example, the word is used in Acts 8:39 to describe Philip's supernatural removal from Gaza to Caesarea. The word is also used by Paul in 2 Corinthians 12:2–4 to describe Paul's being caught up into the third heaven. Thus, there is no doubt that Paul is using the word *harpazo* in 1 Thessalonians 4 to describe the physical removal of people from the earth to heaven.[2]

How will the unbelievers explain the disappearance of millions of people from the earth? It is only conjecture but possibly the Rapture will coincide with some great international disaster that will signal the beginning of the Tribulation and will be a catalyst for a world dictator who promises to bring order out of chaos.

4. Our bodies will be transformed.

Another common question about the Rapture concerns the nature of our new bodies. Specifically, how can deteriorating corpses and even the bodies of living Christians ever enter the kingdom of God? Glad you asked!

There is one more essential ingredient of the Rapture that Paul explains in 1 Corinthians 15:50–55.

Allow me to paraphrase verse 50:

"Here's a simple fact of life. You can't enter into heaven in your present bodies. That which is temporal cannot enter that which is eternal."

So what is the solution to this dilemma? Paul says that at the Rapture our bodies will experience a radical transformation:

Behold, I tell you a mystery; we will not all sleep, but we will all be changed, in a moment, in the twinkling of an eye, at the last trumpet; for the trumpet will sound, and the dead will be raised imperishable, and we will be changed. For this perishable must put on the imperishable, and this mortal must put on immortality. (1 Corinthians 15:51–54)

As we saw in 1 Thessalonians 4, not every Christian will die ("sleep"). Those Christians who are alive at the Rapture will not taste death; instead, they will be snatched away into heaven. However, every Christian must experience a transformation of his mortal body into an immortal body ("we shall all be changed," 1 Corinthians 15:51). At the Rapture our bodies, as well as the bodies of those who have already died, will be instantly transformed into the type of body Jesus possessed after His resurrection. In many ways these new bodies will be radically superior to our present bodies; but in other ways, they will be similar to our present bodies. We will explore these similarities and differences in chapter 10.

Recently a viewer of our television program *Pathway to Victory* called with a question: "I have terminal cancer and I know that my children cannot afford a funeral. So I have decided to donate my body to a medical school. However, I found out that once the medical school is finished with my body, they will cremate my remains. Does the Bible condemn cremation?"

I explained to the caller that while traditionally Christians have buried instead of burned their dead, it really does not matter what happens to your physical body after you die. Whether it is lost at sea, burned in a car wreck, blown apart in an airplane accident, or transplanted into someone else's body is irrelevant to God. At the Rapture, God is going to transform the remains of believers into a body that will forever be free of the pain, suffering, and limitations of this life.

THE RAPTURE QUESTION

Throughout history there have been differing views of the Rapture. Since this book is not designed to be a technical treatise on prophecy, I will only briefly summarize the three major views of the Rapture.

1. The Posttribulation Rapture View

Proponents of this position believe that the Church will endure the seven years of the Tribulation, which will precede the Second Coming of Christ. They see the Rapture as different from the Second Coming, but occurring closely to it. Believers will be caught up with Christ in the air and then return with

Christ to earth as described in Revelation 19:14. Advocates of this view argue that it is naive to believe that believers would be exempt from the great suffering described in Revelation 6–19. Furthermore, they argue that the book of Revelation describes believers who are present on the earth during the Tribulation and are martyred for their faith. If these believers are not the Church, then who are they?

2. The Midtribulation Rapture View

Others believe that the Rapture will occur after the first three-and-a-half years of the seven-year Tribulation. They maintain that the first half of the Tribulation, when the Church is still present on earth, will be relatively peaceful. It is only after the first three-and-a-half years that the world dictator known as Antichrist will break his peace treaty with Israel, ushering in the period of unparalleled persecution of believers that both Daniel and Jesus predicted (see Daniel 9:27 and Matthew 24:15–28). Thus, given the relative peace that will exist during the first half of the Tribulation, there is no need for a Rapture of the Church until after the first three-and-a-half years.

This viewpoint has some merit. It is true that Antichrist does not begin his persecution of believers until the final half of the Tribulation. It is also true that the Bible identifies the final half of the Tribulation (forty-two months or 1,260 days) as the time of intense turmoil and persecution (see Daniel 9:27 and Revelation 11:2–3; 13:5).

But there are also two major problems with the Midtribulation Rapture view. First, it is very difficult to fit all of the events of the Tribulation (discussed in the next chapter) into the final three-and-a-half years. Although the majority of judgments do occur in the final half of the Tribulation, some of them appear to begin before then. Second, if the Church is present at the beginning of the seven years of Tribulation, why is there no mention of the Church in Revelation 6–19?

A popular variation of the Midtribulation Rapture view is the "Pre-Wrath Rapture," first proposed by Robert Van Campen and popularized by Marvin Rosenthal in his book *The Pre-Wrath Rapture of the Church*. According to this theory, Christians will experience the first portion of the Tribulation, which will be characterized by persecution inflicted by Satan and his minions. However, Christians will be raptured prior to the opening of the seventh seal judgment (Revelation 8) and therefore escape God's wrath against the earth. This theory depends upon a distinction between man's (or Satan's) wrath and God's wrath.

However, there are three major problems with this view as well. First, Revelation 5–6 clearly teaches that these beginning seal judgments are God's judgment against the earth as illustrated by the fact that it is the Lamb of God (Jesus Christ) who breaks open the seals (Revelation 6:1). Second, if the Church is present on earth to experience these seal judgments, why is the Church not mentioned in Revelation 6? Finally, as we will see in the next chapter, Daniel 9 and other passages of Scripture view the entire Tribulation as lasting seven years, not just three-and-a-half years.

If the Church is on earth during any portion of these seven years, then it means that the Church will experience God's wrath—something that the Church has been promised it will not have to endure (Romans 8:1).

3. The Pretribulation Rapture View

The prefix *pre-* means "before." Those of us who believe in a Pretribulation Rapture maintain that the Rapture will occur before the beginning of the seven-year Tribulation. I once heard someone say, "I don't know which is the correct view: pre, mid, or post. But I would prefer to be on the first flight going out!" Wouldn't you as well? I am convinced that all Christians are going to be on that "first flight out" because of four key reasons.

The purpose of the Tribulation. As we have already seen, the twofold purpose of the Tribulation is the redemption of Israel and the condemnation of unbelievers. Thus, there is no reason for the Church to be present during the Tribulation.

At our weekly staff meetings, I address the entire staff about topics that concern all of us. But if I have an issue or problem that needs to be brought to the attention of a smaller group or an individual, I will dismiss the rest of the staff and deal privately with those concerned. Why? Not only for efficiency, but for group morale. I have discovered that no one benefits from a general "bawling out" by the pastor. It is much more effective (not to mention Christian!) to rebuke those needing to be corrected as privately as possible.

The same principle applies to the Tribulation. As we will see in more detail in the next chapter, the purpose of the Tribulation is for the correction of Israel and for the judgment of unbelievers. There is no need for the Church to be on earth for those seven years.

The lack of reference to the Church in Revelation 6–18. In Revelation 1–5 the Church is prominent. Beginning in Revelation 19 we see the Church returning with Jesus Christ to earth. But in the detailed description of the horrendous judgments of the Tribulation (Revelation 6–18) there is no mention of the Church. Why? The most obvious reason is because the Church is not present on earth during that horrific period of time.

The teaching of Revelation 3:10. The Lord told John to write this message to the church at Philadelphia:

"Because you have kept the word of My perseverance, I also will keep you from the hour of testing, that hour which is about to come upon the whole world, to test those who dwell on the earth."

The Lord is promising to deliver the Church from (the Greek preposition *ek* means "out of") a universal period of testing "which is about to come upon the whole world." Then, beginning in the next chapter, John begins describing the prelude to that worldwide testing known as the Tribulation. Thus, it is clear that the Lord was promising not only the church at Philadelphia, but all believers that they would be delivered "out of" the Tribulation.

The promise of God that believers will be spared His condemnation. Obviously, believers of every age have endured times of testing. Jesus clearly stated, "In the world you have tribulation"

(John 16:33). Jesus was not referring to the seven-year Tribulation described in Revelation 6–19, but to the difficulties all Christians would face as a result of living in a sin-infected world. Some of those hardships Jesus had in mind certainly included persecution for following Him.

Since Jesus first spoke those words, believers in every age have experienced intense suffering for their faith. The writer of Hebrews describes the plight of Christ-followers just several decades after the Lord made His prediction of suffering:

> They were stoned, they were sawn in two, they were tempted, they were put to death with the sword; they went about in sheepskins, in goatskins, being destitute, afflicted, ill-treated (men of whom the world was not worthy), wandering in deserts and mountains and caves and holes in the ground. (Hebrews 11:37–38)

Two thousand years later, followers of Jesus Christ are still being persecuted for their faith. Although American Christians have been immune (so far) from imprisonment and martyrdom, Christians around the globe are experiencing intense suffering for their faith. Hundreds of thousands of Chinese Christians are detained in work camps each year so that they can participate in a "re-education through labor" program. Christians in Africa and the Middle East are regularly being murdered by Islamic extremists. More Christians died as martyrs during the twentieth century alone than in all other centuries combined.

In addition to persecution, Christians are also subject to sickness, the breakdown of relationships, and the everyday heartaches that come from living in a fallen world. In John 16:33 Jesus was simply saying that every Christian will suffer "tribulation" whether it comes in the form of specific persecution or general travails.

But this kind of universal "tribulation" all residents of planet earth—believers and unbelievers—experience is very different from the suffering that will characterize the final seven years of this current earth's history known as the Tribulation. The distinguishing characteristic of the Tribulation is that it is a time when God will pour out His wrath on an unbelieving world. Those living on the earth during this period of time will experience God's direct judgment for their disobedience, and God has promised to spare believers from that wrath. Paul assured the Roman Christians that "therefore there is now no condemnation for those who are in Christ Jesus" (Romans 8:1).

God took all of the wrath that you and I deserve and poured it out on His Son as He hung on the cross. If Christians must suffer the judgment of God at some future time in history, then the death of Jesus Christ was both ineffective and unnecessary.

I remember hearing the story of a group of cowboys who were caught in the middle of a raging prairie fire. No way of escape was possible. As the fire approached, one of the men said, "Quick, let's burn the ground around us." At first the others could not believe such a ludicrous idea until the cowboy explained, "The fire cannot come where it has already been." We are protected from the future wrath of God because that condemnation has already been experienced by His Son. The fire cannot come where it has already been. That is the strongest argument I know for a Pretribulation Rapture.

SO WHAT?

How does the certainty of a future Rapture affect my life today? The apostle Paul encouraged Titus to be "looking for the blessed hope and the appearing of the glory of our great God and Savior, Christ Jesus" (Titus 2:13). In other words, we should live with the expectation that at any moment the Rapture could occur. Although there are numerous prophecies that need to be fulfilled before the Second Coming, there are *no* prophecies that must be fulfilled prior to the Rapture. It could happen next year, next week, or before you finish this chapter. While that truth does not mean we should quit our jobs, move to a commune, or max out our credit cards and go to Disney World, we should live each day with the realization that at any time the trumpet could sound, the clouds could part, and the Lord could appear for His own.

Earlier I cited 1 Corinthians 15:52, which speaks of the imminence of the Rapture:

"in a moment, in the twinkling of an eye, at the last trumpet; for the trumpet will sound, and the dead will be raised imperishable, and we will be changed."

What is the significance of "the last trumpet"? Whenever Roman soldiers were about to break camp and march to a new location, there would always be three blasts of the trumpets. The first blast meant "strike your tents and prepare to depart"; the second blast meant "fall in line"; and the final blast meant "march away." I believe that God has already sounded the first trumpet. He has reminded us that we need to strike our tents and be living as strangers and aliens in this world which is about to be destroyed. He has also sounded the second blast telling us to be sober and on the alert for His appearance. All we are waiting for is that last blast of the trumpet at which time we will march away into the presence of our Commander.

Chapter Five

||||||||||||||||||||||||||||||||||||||||||||

WHEN ALL HELL
BREAKS LOOSE

T ragic events happening in the Middle East—especially in
Israel—continue to be a constant focus of world news on
a daily basis. Much of the news coming out of Israel graphically
shows suicide bombings, terrorist attacks, and ongoing preparations for war due to the constant threats this small democracy
experiences from her neighbors. The Jewish leaders, the Jewish
people, and much of the world longs for a peaceful solution to
the long period of conflict going on between Israel and the Arab
world surrounding her. While past attempts to find peaceful
solutions for the problems in this region remain temporary and
elusive, the Bible indicates that true peace will not come from
human efforts, but only when Jesus the Messiah sets up His kingdom on the earth.

From the book of Revelation, we discover that prior to a lasting peace coming to this area and the entire world, there will be a
chaotic seven-year period in world history commonly referred to

as the Great Tribulation. It will be a time of unprecedented calamity precipitated by political unrest and natural disasters. But the most distinguishing characteristic of this period is that God will pour out His unrelenting wrath upon the inhabitants of the earth.

In this chapter we are going to survey the major events of the Great Tribulation. But before we do that, we need to understand God's purpose for the Tribulation. And the place to begin is the book of Daniel.

GOD'S MAN IN BABYLON

Daniel was a Jewish teenager who was taken captive by the Babylonian king Nebuchadnezzar in the sixth century BC. The first six chapters of the book of Daniel record Daniel's remarkable ministry as God's representative during those seventy years of Israel's exile. The final six chapters, however, are prophetic. As you can imagine, Daniel and the Jewish exiles were severely depressed over being uprooted from their homeland and being planted in a strange and pagan culture. The Israelites must have wondered . . .

- Has God forgotten the covenant He made with our   father Abraham?
- Why would God allow a pagan nation to conquer the people of God?
- Will we ever return to our homeland?
- Where is Israel's promised Deliverer when we need Him most?

In response to those questions, God gave Daniel a series of visions that allowed this young prophet/statesman to peer down the corridor of history and see how God would fulfill His promise to His people. After a period of prayer and fasting, Daniel heard this message from the angel Gabriel:

> O Daniel, I have now come forth to give you insight with understanding. At the beginning of your supplications the command was issued, and I have come to tell you, for you are highly esteemed; so give heed to the message and gain understanding of the vision. Seventy weeks have been decreed for your people and your holy city, to finish the transgression, to make an end of sin, to make atonement for iniquity, to bring in everlasting righteousness, to seal up vision and prophecy and to anoint the most holy place. (Daniel 9:22–24)

As the first portion of Daniel 9 illustrates, Daniel was extremely concerned about Israel's need to return to Jerusalem, so that God's reputation would not be damaged among the Gentile nations. If God were incapable of fulfilling His promise of a secure home for Israel, then He was not a God worthy of worship. Responding to Daniel's sincere concern, God gives the prophet more than he bargained for! In these few verses, God outlines for Daniel His final plan for Israel.

Gabriel announces that there are "seventy weeks" left for God to fulfill His purpose for Israel. The word "weeks" is a poor translation of the Hebrew text. The word can be translated "sevens." Within "seventy sevens," God would complete His earthly plan for Israel. There is ample evidence to support the idea that God is talking about years instead of weeks, especially since earlier in chapter 9 Daniel had been referring to the number of years until Israel's return to Jerusalem (see Daniel 9:1–2). Thus, I believe that the term "seventy sevens" can be interpreted as seventy weeks of years or 490 years (each week representing seven years). It is the only interpretation that fits the context of this chapter.

Gabriel announces that God will use these 490 years:

- "To finish the transgression." This is most likely a reference to the end of Israel's rebellion and unbelief.
- "To make an end of sin." This phrase probably refers to an end to the sacrificial system.
- "To make atonement for iniquity." I believe this phrase refers to the sacrificial death of Messiah which provided the ultimate atonement (meaning "covering") for our sin.
- "To bring in everlasting righteousness." This phrase refers to the establishment of Messiah's rule over the earth as prophesied in Isaiah 11.
- "To seal up vision and prophecy." Once Messiah's rule is established, there will no longer be a need for prophecy (or for books on prophecy!).
- "To anoint the most holy place." The "holy place" is obviously a reference to the temple that had been destroyed

during the Babylonian invasion. This phrase anticipates a rebuilding of the temple and a re-establishment of the sacrificial system.

The question is *which* temple? Historically, Zerubbabel rebuilt the temple in 516 BC after Israel's return from Babylon. That temple, however, after being enlarged by King Herod, was later destroyed by the Romans in AD 70.

As we will see in a moment, during the first half of the coming seven-year Tribulation, Israel will once again be offering sacrifices, necessitating the rebuilding of the temple. Furthermore, sacrifices will be offered during the Millennium, requiring yet another temple. Thus, this phrase in Daniel may be a reference to Zerubbabel's temple or to some future temple.

Currently there is much talk in Israel about the rebuilding of the temple. In September of 1998 a conference in Jerusalem calling for the rebuilding of the temple attracted 2,000 participants. At the Treasuries of the Temple museum in Jerusalem, one can see a list of projects being undertaken in anticipation of the rebuilding of the temple including the creation of the priestly garments as described in the Exodus 39.[1]

The Temple Institute in Jerusalem maintains a website detailing preparations and progress on rebuilding the Jewish temple. Some actual sacred temple vessels have already been created by craftsmen for use in this anticipated temple. In 2012, a special workshop was inaugurated in order to begin manufacturing the priestly garments.[2]

GOD'S STOPWATCH

Twenty-five hundred years have elapsed since Gabriel revealed this outline of future events to Daniel. From Daniel's perspective, all six of these events would occur at some future date. From our vantage point looking back, we see that some of these events revealed to Daniel have already been fulfilled, such as Christ's atonement for our sins at His first coming. Other events are yet to be fulfilled such as Christ's perfect rule over the earth when He comes again. Yet Gabriel's message was that all of the events would be fulfilled in a 490-year period of time. So how do we reconcile Gabriel's message that all of these events would occur within a 490-year period of time with the fact that more than 2,500 years have passed and only some of these prophecies have been fulfilled?

Imagine that God is holding a stopwatch that begins with 490 years. From the time God presses the "start" button until the clock ticks all the way down to "0" years, all of the above described events will take place. That was Gabriel's message to Daniel. A natural question would be, "When does God press the 'start' button?" Gabriel answers that question in verse 25:

So you are to know and discern that from the issuing of a decree to restore and rebuild Jerusalem until Messiah the Prince there will be seven weeks and sixty-two weeks. (Daniel 9:25)

The 490 years began ticking away, Gabriel says, whenever the Jews were permitted to leave Babylon and return to rebuild Jerusalem. Although Cyrus authorized the rebuilding of the temple in 538 BC, it was the Persian ruler Artaxerxes Longimanus who issued the actual decree to rebuild the city of Jerusalem on March 14, 445 BC (Nehemiah 2:5). So on that day, God's final countdown of 490 years began during which He would complete His plan for Israel.

God's Stopwatch
Daniel 9:24-27
490 years

7 years remaining

483 years elapsed
March 14, 445 BC - April 2, 32 AD

Now, here is where it gets really interesting! Gabriel says that from the time that the decree to rebuild Jerusalem is issued until "Messiah the Prince" there will be a period of sixty-nine weeks of years (seven weeks + sixty-two weeks = sixty-nine weeks of years) or 483 years. I believe that the title "Messiah the Prince" refers to Jesus' triumphal entry into Jerusalem on Palm Sunday, as prophesied in Zechariah 9:9. Thus, Gabriel says 483 years will elapse between the decree to rebuild Jerusalem until the presentation of the Messiah on Palm Sunday. Did that happen?

Dr. J. Dwight Pentecost has demonstrated that exactly 483 years elapsed between these two signal events. Using the Jewish calendar of 360 days, the edict from Artaxerxes was issued on the first of Nisan (March 14, 445 BC). Christ rode into Jerusalem on the back of a colt (see Matthew 21:1–11) on the tenth of Nisan (April 2) AD 32. Factoring in some of the irregularities of the Jewish calendar, Dr. Pentecost demonstrates that the time between these two signal events is exactly 483 years.[3]

But Gabriel revealed to Daniel that there will be a gap between those first 483 years and the final seven years during which God will fulfill His plans for Israel:

> Then *after* the sixty-two weeks [plus seven weeks mentioned
> in 9:25 for a total of sixty-nine weeks] the Messiah will be
> cut off and have nothing, and the people of the prince who
> is to come will destroy the city and the sanctuary. And its
> end will come with a flood; even to the end there will be war;
> desolations are determined (Daniel 9:26; emphasis mine).

After Israel rejected Christ and crucified the Messiah, God hit the "pause" button of that imaginary stopwatch. How do we know that? Notice that all of the events in Daniel 9:26 (the death of Messiah and the destruction of Jerusalem and the Temple) occur *after* the sixty-nine weeks or 483 years and before the final "week" or seven years in Daniel 9:27. Four hundred and eighty-three years had elapsed; only seven remain on the stopwatch. As we saw in the previous chapter, this "pause" in God's program with Israel is the time we are living in now—the Church Age. During this time God has *temporarily* turned aside from Israel to allow Gentiles to become heirs of the Abrahamic Covenant. But God is not through with Israel yet. Remember Romans 11:25?

> For I do not want you, brethren, to be uninformed of this mystery—so that you will not be wise in your own estimation—that a partial hardening has happened to Israel until the fullness of the Gentiles has come in.

There are still seven years remaining on God's stopwatch. When will those final seven years began ticking away? Gabriel again provides the answer:

> And he [the great world dictator we call Antichrist] will make a firm covenant with the many for one week, but in the middle of the week he will put a stop to sacrifice and grain offering; and on the wing of abominations will come one who makes desolate, even until a complete destruction, one that is decreed, is poured out on the one who makes desolate. (Daniel 9:27)

The final seven-year countdown begins with this great world dictator establishing a peace treaty with the nation of Israel. Halfway through those seven years (commonly known as the Tribulation), this ruler will betray Israel and instigate a period of unparalleled persecution against the people of God. These final three-and-a-half years (called a time of "great tribulation" by Jesus in Matthew 24:21) will climax with the return of Christ and the establishment of His kingdom.

THE DAY OF THE LORD

This seven-year period of time during which God deals with the nation of Israel, as well as the unbelieving world, is known by a variety of titles: "the time of Jacob's distress," "Daniel's seventieth week," or "the Tribulation." But the most common biblical name for this seven-year period is "the day of the Lord." Without exception, the term *the Day of the Lord* refers to God's judgment against both Israel and the unbelieving world and will culminate in Christ's return and rule over the earth. Look at how some of the Old Testament prophets described the Day of the Lord:

Alas for the day! For the day of the LORD is near,
And it will come as destruction from the Almighty.
(Joel 1:15)

Alas, you who are longing for the day of the LORD,
For what purpose will the day of the LORD be to you?

It will be darkness and not light . . .
Will not the day of the LORD be darkness instead of light,
Even gloom with no brightness in it? (Amos 5:18, 20)

Near is the great day of the LORD,
Near and coming very quickly;
Listen, the day of the LORD! . . .
A day of wrath is that day,
A day of trouble and distress,
A day of destruction and desolation,
A day of darkness and gloom,
A day of clouds and thick darkness. (Zephaniah 1:14–15)

The apostle Paul also discussed both the chronology and the characteristics of the Day of the Lord in 1 Thessalonians 4–5. After explaining the Rapture of the Church in 1 Thessalonians 4:13–18, Paul continues by describing the event that will take place after the Rapture—the Day of the Lord:

Now as to the times and the epochs, brethren, you have no need of anything to be written to you. For you yourselves know full well that the day of the Lord will come just like a thief in the night. While they are saying, "Peace and safety!" then destruction will come upon them suddenly like labor pains upon a woman with child, and they will not escape. But you, brethren, are not in darkness, that the day would overtake you like a thief. (1 Thessalonians 5:1–4)

These four brief verses reveal three important truths about the Day of the Lord:

1. The Day of the Lord follows the Rapture of the Church. The explanation of the Day of the Lord in 1 Thessalonians 5 comes *after* the description of the Rapture in 1 Thessalonians 4:13–18.
2. The Day of the Lord is a time of judgment upon unbelievers (1 Thessalonians 5:3).
3. Christians need not fear the Day of the Lord (1 Thessalonians 5:4).

MAJOR EVENTS OF THE TRIBULATION

The most detailed description of the events of the Day of the Lord (or "Great Tribulation") is found in Revelation 6–19. Since it would be impossible to detail this entire period of time in one chapter, allow me to summarize the major events of the Tribulation, using Daniel's division of a beginning, middle, and end (Daniel 9:27).

Act I: The Beginning of the Tribulation

Three major events will characterize the first three-and-a-half years of the period known as the Tribulation.

1. THE RISE OF ANTICHRIST

When the 1993 Mideast peace treaty was ratified, one popular radio evangelist announced that the seven years of Tribulation had begun. Obviously he was wrong, but why did he make such a

pronouncement? According to Daniel's outline of this final "week"
of years, the signal event that begins this final period prior to
Christ's return will be a peace treaty that Antichrist will make with
Israel (Daniel 9:27). I believe that the Rapture of the Church may
coincide with some cataclysmic world event that will precipitate a
universal clamor for a great leader to unite the nations. A disaster
such as a nuclear accident, a giant asteroid, a financial meltdown,
or another world war could be the catalyst that would set the stage
for this great world leader. However, most probably a crisis in the
Middle East will bring Antichrist to the world stage.

In our nation's recent past we have seen Secretary of State Henry
Kissinger, President Jimmy Carter, and President Bill Clinton enjoy
tremendous world acclaim for brokering peace agreements in the
Middle East that ultimately fell apart. It is easy to see how a future
leader could win the respect and devotion of the world if he were
able to establish what was perceived to be a lasting solution to the
conflict in the Middle East—especially if that conflict had precipitated a worldwide economic crisis that would naturally arise from
any disruption of oil production.

A synthesis of verses reveals a number of interesting facts about
the Antichrist:

1. *He will come to power after Christians are removed from the
   earth according to 2 Thessalonians 2:6-9* (although it is certainly possible that he could be alive today).
2. *He most likely will be a Gentile.* Revelation 13:1 describes him
   as coming out of the "sea" (a common biblical expression

describing Gentiles though it could also refer to the constant churning of the political world).

3. *He will rule over a revived Roman empire that will apparently be in the form of a ten-nation confederacy.* Daniel 9:26–27 identifies those who kill Messiah as "the people of the prince who is to come" and as the ones who destroyed the temple—a direct reference to the Romans who invaded Jerusalem and destroyed the Temple in AD 70.

I remember when I was in high school hearing the rumor that President John F. Kennedy was still alive, living on some remote island in Greece, and was going to reemerge as the Antichrist. Proponents of this theory pointed to Revelation 13:3:

> I saw one of his heads as if it had been slain, and his fatal wound was healed. And the whole earth was amazed and followed after the beast.

However, I believe a more plausible explanation is that this verse is referring to a political resurrection of the beast's empire (Rome) rather than the physical resurrection of Antichrist himself. The world will be amazed that the Roman empire, thought to be dead, will be resurrected in the form of this ten-nation confederacy presided over by Antichrist.

4. *He will oppose the people of God and attempt to change the laws of God without opposition* (Daniel 7:25). This future world leader will launch an unprecedented persecution against God's

people, trying to "wear down the saints" (Daniel 7:25). Daniel also prophesied that this future world leader would "intend to make alterations in times and in laws" (Daniel 7:25).

For the first time in history a president of our country has openly proposed altering one of society's (not to mention God's) most fundamental laws: that marriage should be between a man and a woman. While I am not suggesting that President Obama is the Antichrist, the fact that he was able to propose such a sweeping change in God's law and still win reelection by a comfortable margin illustrates how a future world leader will be able to oppose God's laws without any repercussions.

It is significant that the Antichrist will be able to persecute God's people, seek to change God's laws, and usurp people's freedom of worship and commerce without any recorded opposition. How could that happen? The only explanation is that prior to the appearance of Antichrist, people will have already become so numb to immorality, apathetic and even sympathetic to the persecution of religious "extremists" (which will be the new term for committed Christians), and conditioned to the government's usurpation of personal freedom, that Antichrist's rise to power will go unchallenged.

2. THE RISE OF THE FALSE PROPHET

Assisting the rise and rule of Antichrist will be a man, empowered by Satan, commonly referred to as "the false prophet." He will probably be a religious leader who will head a world church described as a "harlot" in Revelation. This apostate church will have the appearance of a legitimate church, but will deny the basic tenets of Christianity. Some have tried to identify this false church as an already existing religious group or denomination. However, this future world church most probably will be an amalgamation of different religious beliefs. Given our culture's increasing disdain for the absolute truth claims of historic Christianity, it is not hard to see how—in the name of world peace—a new syncretic religion could develop that is a mixture of some of the more appealing aspects of some of the world's most popular religions: one part Christian, two parts Islam, sprinkled with New Age transcendentalism. Even today there are numerous churches that profess belief in the Bible, Jesus Christ, and the cross. And yet, when you peel away the religious trappings of these churches, you find a belief system that denies the essence of Christianity: that salvation is through faith alone in Christ's sacrificial death.

During the first three-and-a-half years of the seven-year Tribulation, the false prophet will use his religious influence to promote Antichrist's agenda. However, after the first three-and-a-half years of the Tribulation, Antichrist will decide that he no longer needs this false church and will destroy it, directing all worship toward himself:

> And the ten horns which you saw, and the beast, these will hate the harlot and will make her desolate and naked, and will eat her flesh and will burn her up with fire. (Revelation 17:16)

After the destruction of this apostate church, the false prophet will move from the religious world to the political world to assist Antichrist in achieving his goals. Specifically, the false prophet will control world commerce by limiting the purchase of goods to those who are willing to demonstrate their allegiance to Antichrist by carrying the number 666:

> And he [the false prophet] causes all, the small and the great, and the rich and the poor, and the free men and the slaves, to be given a mark on their right hand or on their forehead, and he provides that no one will be able to buy or to sell, except the one who has the mark, either the name of the beast or the number of his name. . . . And the number of his name is six hundred and sixty-six. (Revelation 13:16–18)

Is it really plausible that people would readily accept having a mark placed on their bodies in order to participate in financial transactions as Revelation predicts? Think about this: Until just a few years ago, having a tattoo was considered degrading or something only lower-class people or drunken sailors would do to alter their bodies. Now, among young adults and the well-to-do celebrity elite, tattooing has become fashionable. With the use of bar codes already used for scanning on most products, it would be easy for people to have a personalized bar code tattooed on their hands or foreheads.

In the same way that people readily accept the government's edict that they cannot get on an airplane without passing through a scanning device (not to mention a highly personal pat down by a TSA employee!), it is understandable how people would accept the government's mandate that they must carry a mark on their body if they wish to engage in commerce (the rationale for such a personal bar code could be efficiency, taxation, or national security).

In a similar manner, a biochip with personal information can now be inserted under the skin of animals and people for identification purposes. In 2008, the journal *New Scientist* published an article detailing how affluent Mexicans, worried of soaring kidnappings in their country, were having tiny transmitters inserted under their skin so that satellites could help them be found in the event they were abducted by drug lords or other criminals.[4]

The technology, as well as the precedent, already exists that will make the Antichrist's mandate easy to implement.

3. THE SEALING OF THE 144,000

Another important event during the first three-and-a-half years of the Tribulation is the calling out of 144,000 missionaries who will be responsible for the conversion of many Jews and Gentiles during the Tribulation. They are supernaturally sealed and therefore protected by God from destruction by Antichrist. The apostle John describes a voice from heaven he heard saying,

> "Do not harm the earth or the sea or the trees until we have sealed the bond-servants of our God on their foreheads."
> And I heard the number of those who were sealed, one

hundred and forty-four thousand sealed from every tribe
of the sons of Israel. (Revelation 7:3–4)

Who are these 144,000 individuals who are supernaturally protected by God during the Tribulation? The Seventh
Day Adventists believe it is a reference to their members who
are observing the Sabbath when Christ returns. The Jehovah's
Witnesses claim that John had their group in mind here.
Christians who believe in a Posttribulation Rapture believe the
144,000 represent the Church, which they believe will be on
earth during the Tribulation.

But such speculation is unnecessary because John clearly identifies
the 144,000. He explains they are Jews from each of the twelve tribes
of Israel (see Revelation 7:5–8). These Jewish evangelists will be saved
after the Rapture and will share the message of Christ with people
from every nation. Many Jews and Gentiles will be converted during
the Tribulation but will experience great persecution or even death at
the hands of Antichrist. After detailing the call of these 144,000 missionaries, John describes the result of their ministry: a multitude of
converts from every nation who are martyred by Antichrist:

After these things I looked, and behold, a great multitude which no one could count, from every nation and all
tribes and peoples and tongues, standing before the throne
and before the Lamb, clothed in white robes, and palm
branches were in their hands; . . . "These are the ones who
come out of the great tribulation, and they have washed

their robes and made them white in the blood of the Lamb." (Revelation 7:9, 14)

I am often asked this question: "If it is still possible for people to be saved after the Rapture, why not wait until then to see if all of this stuff is really true?" The fact that many will be saved after the Rapture is no excuse for delaying one's decision to trust in Christ. Think about it. If a person is not willing to be saved in this age in which many Christians (at least in America) are spared persecution, why would they be willing to be saved during the Tribulation when they will have to endure tremendous hardships for their faith? Nevertheless, some during the Tribulation will risk their lives in order to obtain eternal life.

The rise of Antichrist and the false prophet, along with the sealing of the 144,000 Jewish evangelists, will be the major events of the first three-and-a-half years of the Tribulation. All indications are that this first half of the Tribulation will be relatively tranquil. "Peace and safety" will be the watchwords of this period (1 Thessalonians 5:3). Antichrist will be hailed as a hero because he has achieved what was thought to be the unachievable: peace in the Middle East. But halfway through the seven years, Antichrist will do an about-face that will plunge the world into its darkest hour.

Act II: The Midpoint of the Tribulation

The prophet Daniel, the apostle John, and the Lord Jesus Christ all prophesied a key event that would take place halfway through the seven-year Tribulation. After the first three-and-a-half years,

Antichrist will break the peace treaty he brokered with Israel and will begin persecuting the Jews, as well as those who will become Christians during that time. Daniel, Matthew, and Revelation all give us great insight into this turning point in the Tribulation.

From the book of Daniel we learn that this ruler of the revived Roman empire will break his covenant with Israel during the middle of the "week" of years, will become an adversary of Israel, and will make Jerusalem his headquarters during the final three-and-a-half years of his reign of terror:

> And he will make a firm covenant with the many for one week, but in the middle of the week he will put a stop to sacrifice and grain offering; and on the wing of abominations will come one who makes desolate, even until a complete destruction, one that is decreed, is poured out on the one who makes desolate. (Daniel 9:27)

> I kept looking, and that horn was waging war with the saints and overpowering them. (Daniel 7:21)

> He will pitch the tents of his royal pavilion between the seas and the beautiful Holy Mountain; yet he will come to his end, and no one will help him. (Daniel 11:45)

The book of Revelation reveals that the duration of Antichrist's persecution of Israel is three-and-a-half years (forty-two months, or 1,260 days):

Leave out the court which is outside the temple and do not measure it, for it has been given to the nations [Gentiles under the rule of Antichrist]; and they will tread under foot the holy city for forty-two months. (Revelation 11:2)

And I will grant authority to my two witnesses, and they will prophesy for twelve hundred and sixty days, clothed in sackcloth. (Revelation 11:3)

There was given to him [Antichrist] a mouth speaking arrogant words and blasphemies, and authority to act for forty-two months was given to him. (Revelation 13:5)

Jesus Christ also taught that the last three-and-a-half years of the Tribulation would begin with Antichrist's turning against Israel and would conclude with His own return to earth:

Therefore when you see the abomination of desolation which was spoken of through Daniel the prophet, standing in the holy place (let the reader understand), then those who are in Judea must flee to the mountains. . . . But immediately after the tribulation of those days . . . the sign of the Son of Man will appear in the sky, and then all the tribes of the earth will mourn, and they will see the Son of Man coming on the clouds of the sky with power and great glory. (Matthew 24:15–16, 29–30)

Act III: Earth's Final Hours

Jesus described these final three-and-a-half years as the "great tribulation, such as has not occurred since the beginning of the world until now, nor ever will. Unless those days had been cut short, no life would have been saved; but for the sake of the elect those days will be cut short" (Matthew 24:21–22). A study of the different judgments God pours out on the earth during this period of time will help you understand why Jesus would make such a statement. God's judgments against the earth (described in Revelation 6–19) will come in a series of three judgments known as the seal judgments, the trumpet judgments, and the bowl judgments. Space will only allow for a summary of each of these three judgments.

1. THE SEAL JUDGMENTS

The seal judgments, described in Revelation 6, began with the rise of Antichrist (6:1–2), and include war (6:3–4), famine (6:5–6), death from the famine that will destroy one-fourth of the world's population (6:7–8), martyrdom of those converted after the Rapture of the Church (6:9–11), and tremendous cosmological disturbances (6:12–17). The final seal judgment actually contains all of the trumpet judgments described in Revelation 8:2–11:5.

2. THE TRUMPET JUDGMENTS

No one can be dogmatic as to whether the seal judgments occur during the first half or the final half of the Tribulation. Persuasive arguments can be made for either viewpoint. However, when we come to the next series of judgments known as the trumpet judgments (described in Revelation 8–9), it is evident that we are in the final three-and-a-half years of the Tribulation.

The first four trumpet judgments are directed against nature, much like the plagues God pronounced upon Egypt during the days of Moses. During the first trumpet judgment, God uses a mixture of hail and fire to destroy one-third of the earth's vegetation. The second trumpet judgment involves "something like a great mountain burning with fire" falling into the sea (Revelation 8:8). Could this be a reference to a giant asteroid? Our solar system is full of asteroids or space rubble. Essentially, asteroids are chunks of rock ranging from a few feet long to several miles in diameter. The surface of our moon has been scarred with craters from past impacts by asteroids and meteors—asteroids that have broken into smaller pieces.

Scientists claim that sixty-five million years ago a five-mile-wide asteroid struck the Yucatan Peninsula, destroying the dinosaurs (I don't know whether that happened or not since I wasn't there!). In 1908, a two-hundred-foot rock exploded over Siberia, wiping out thousands of square miles of forest. More recently, in February 2013, a meteor blazed through the sky and exploded over central Russia. The aftershock from this explosion injured hundreds of people as a result of broken glass and falling debris.[5]

Today, organizations like Spacewatch and Near-Earth Tracking comb the skies for these objects that could one day destroy the planet.[6] Whatever "the great mountain" is, this judgment destroys one-third of all marine life and one-third of all the ships, resulting in ecological and economic disaster.

A falling star destroys one third of the earth's freshwater supply during the third trumpet judgment (8:10–11). The fourth trumpet judgment involves a disruption of the rotation pattern of the earth and moon, causing wide fluctuations in temperatures (8:12).

During the fifth trumpet judgment, described in Revelation 9:1–12, Satan (the "star from heaven") unleashes demonic tormentors to persecute mankind, except those who have been sealed by God. These torturers are described as locusts with a sting comparable to scorpions; but their power is derived from Satan. The pain they inflict will be so horrible that people will beg to die but will be unable to do so (Revelation 9:6). Imagine for a moment the most severe pain you have ever experienced (for me it was a kidney stone). Now, imagine experiencing that pain—without any relief— for five months. That will be the fifth trumpet judgment against the earth.

The sixth trumpet judgment involves the assembling of a massive army of two hundred million soldiers (Revelation 9:16) who are later described as coming from the east (Revelation 16:12–16). We should probably understand this army as a human army that is demonically empowered by four demons (described as "angels" in Revelation 9:15). The battle described beginning in Revelation 9:18 may be the beginning of the war we refer to as Armageddon, which could extend for several years until the return of Christ.

John noted that this war kills one third of mankind (Revelation 9:18). When you combine this number with those already killed as a result of the fourth seal judgment (one-fourth of the earth according to

Revelation 6:8), it means that one-half of the world's population has been destroyed. Now we can see why Jesus said that unless these days had been cut short, no one would have survived.

3. THE BOWL JUDGMENTS

Like the seventh seal judgment, the seventh trumpet judgment includes all of the next series of judgments: the bowl judgments as described in Revelation 16:1–21. As we read through these judgments, several facts are obvious. First, they are very similar to the trumpet judgments described in Revelation 8–9. It seems like—to use Yogi Berra's expression—"déjà vu all over again." But while the trumpet judgments affected only a portion of the earth, these judgments impact the entire planet.

The reader also senses the rapidity of these judgments. They probably occur over the span of just a few days and lead up to the return of Jesus Christ. The final bowl judgment is especially severe:

> Then the seventh angel poured out his bowl upon the air, and a loud voice came out of the temple from the throne, saying, "It is done." And there were flashes of lightning and sounds and peals of thunder; and there was a great earthquake, such as there had not been since man came to be upon the earth, so great an earthquake was it, and so mighty. The great city was split into three parts, and the cities of the nations fell. Babylon the great was remembered before God, to give her the cup of the wine of His fierce wrath. (Revelation 16:17–19)

Since this judgment is poured out "upon the air" and is accompanied by "flashes of lightning" and "peals of thunder," some have speculated that John is describing a nuclear explosion. If so, it results in a destruction of Babylon—most likely a reference to whatever city is the seat of Antichrist's power. Babylon was occasionally used as synonym for Rome in the New Testament (see 1 Peter 5:13), but could also be a symbol of some other great city such as London, Paris, or Washington, D.C. Some have even speculated that John was referring to the actual city of Babylon, which the late Iraqi leader Saddam Hussein pledged to restore to the splendor of Nebuchadnezzar.[7] Plans remain underway for the ancient site of the city of Babylon to become a tourist destination. According to a June 28, 2009, article in the United States military newspaper *Stars and Stripes,* the 172nd Infantry Brigade helped to develop a preservation and tourism plan for the area. The State Department and the World Monuments Fund have already committed $700,000 toward this project. It is hoped that the area could draw millions of tourists every year comparable to the visitors of the Egyptian pyramids. Such an extensive project would help fulfill Saddam Hussein's dream and plans for the reemergence of this once great city cut short by his execution.[8]

THE PURPOSE OF THE TRIBULATION

I am regularly accused of being a "hate preacher" for teaching that the only way a person can escape the reality of hell is by trusting in

Jesus Christ for the forgiveness of his or her sins. In response to a recent television interview in which I made that claim, one person wrote on a blog, "I believe in a God of love, not of judgment. If God is so intolerant and cruel that He would dispatch those who don't accept His Son to a place of eternal torment, then I would just as soon be separated from Him for eternity, too."

However, is it possible that God could be both judgmental and loving? Suppose I tell my daughter that if she sticks her finger into an electrical outlet she will die. Am I being judgmental or loving? I am certainly making the judgment that sticking one's finger into a socket is wrong, but I am doing so out of love, not hatred. Warning people of the inevitable consequences of sin and pointing them to Jesus Christ so they can experience God's forgiveness is the most loving thing we can do, especially if it leads them to make the right choice.

God is perfect love *and* He is perfect holiness. His holy nature demands that He judge sin, and He will do just that during the Tribulation:

"For behold, the Lord is about to come out from His place to punish the inhabitants of the earth for their iniquity" (Isaiah 26:21).

But even in the midst of His judgment, we also see God's love. If God were simply interested in annihilating unbelievers, why would He dispatch 144,000 missionaries to proclaim His message of salvation? Never forget that God's ultimate purpose during these final seven years is to bring Israel, as well as the rest of the world, to a saving relationship with Christ. As God said through the prophet Ezekiel,

"As I live!" declares the Lord GOD, "I take no pleasure in the death of the wicked, but rather that the wicked turn from his way and live. Turn back, turn back from your evil ways! Why then will you die, O house of Israel?" (Ezekiel 33:11)

What God desires for Israel and the world at large, He desires for you as well. After writing thousands of pages in his book on church dogmatics, theologian Karl Barth formulated this simple definition of God: "the One who loves." Why does God send tribulation into your life? Because He's angry with you? Because He likes watching you squirm in discomfort? Of course not. If God were interested in getting even with you, He could destroy you with a single word . . . or just a thought. The Creator of the universe so longs for a relationship with you that He will use whatever means necessary to drive you into the arms of the One who loves you.

Chapter Six

|||||||||||||||||||||||||||||||||||||||||

HISTORY'S MOST IMPORTANT EVENT

In January of 1961, a few days before John F. Kennedy was inaugurated as president of the United States, the president-elect invited Billy Graham to spend a day with him in Key Biscayne, Florida. The invitation surprised the evangelist because of Kennedy's well-known dislike for Graham and lack of interest in spiritual matters. After a round of golf, Kennedy and Graham were returning to their hotel when Kennedy stopped the white Lincoln convertible he was driving by the side of the road.

"Billy, do you believe that Jesus Christ is coming back to earth one day?"

"Yes, Mr. President, I certainly do."

"Then why do I hear so little about it?"[1]

The return of Jesus Christ to establish His kingdom is one of the best kept secrets in the world. And, yet, throughout the Bible we hear the constant refrain that Christ is returning to earth to judge the righteous and the unrighteous. In this chapter we will examine . . .

- The events that will precede the Second Coming of Christ.
- The difference between the Rapture and the Second Coming of Christ.
- The reasons for the Second Coming of Christ.

But first . . . a short review of where we have been.

SO FAR . . .

In Genesis 12, God promised to Abraham that He would give him and his descendants a specific land, an enduring nation, and a spiritual blessing that would overflow to all the nations of the world. Despite Israel's continued disobedience, God never wavered in His resolve to fulfill His covenant:

> But I will not break off My lovingkindness from him,
> Nor deal falsely in My faithfulness.
> My covenant I will not violate,
> Nor will I alter the utterance of My lips.
> (Psalm 89:33–34)

When would God's promises to Israel be fulfilled? This question was particularly relevant to the Israelites who had been exiled to Babylon in 586 BC. Uprooted from their homeland, these Israelites began to wonder if God had revoked His covenant with them. To reassure the Israelites of His faithfulness, God gave Daniel four visions concerning Israel's future. In the most remarkable vision,

God actually specified a timetable for fulfilling His promises to the Israelites. From the time Israel returned to Jerusalem to rebuild the city until God's plan for Israel was completed would be a period of 490 years (Daniel 9:24–27).

However, God also revealed to Daniel that there would be a gap between the first 483 years and the final seven years. During that parentheses, in which we are now living, the apostle Paul explained that God is allowing Gentiles to be saved (Romans 11:25). But this parentheses should not be confused with a period. God is not yet finished with Israel; there are seven remaining years left on God's stopwatch. Before this final seven years begins, He is going to remove His Church (those who are saved during this present time period) from the earth in an event known as the Rapture (1 Thessalonians 4:13–18).

The final seven years of God's future program for Israel is called the Tribulation. As we saw in chapter 4, God's purpose for the Tribulation is twofold: (1) to pour out His wrath on unbelievers, and (2) to give unbelieving Israelites and Gentiles one last chance to repent prior to the return of Christ.

While the first three-and-a-half years of the Tribulation will be relatively peaceful, the final half will be marked by Antichrist's reign of terror upon the earth. But Antichrist will not be the only disruptive force in the world during these final years; God will also be unleashing His punishment through a series of judgments directed against the earth's resources and population.

You've probably heard the old saying, "He who calls the shots, takes the shots." That maxim will also apply to Antichrist. Tired of his tyrannical rule that has resulted in worldwide destruction, leaders of other nations will marshal their forces to challenge Antichrist in a war known as Armageddon.

Look Up and Look Out

The setting for Armageddon is found in Revelation 16:

> And I saw coming out of the mouth of the dragon and out of the mouth of the beast and out of the mouth of the false prophet, three unclean spirits like frogs; for they are spirits of demons, performing signs, which go out to the kings of the whole world, to gather them together for the war of the great day of God, the Almighty. . . . And they gathered them together to the place which in Hebrew is called Har-Magedon. (Revelation 16:13–14, 16)

While there are many unanswered questions about this climactic world conflict we call Armageddon, John clearly states that evil spirits proceeding from the Satanic trinity (the dragon=Satan; the beast=Antichrist; and the false prophet=Antichrist's lieutenant) will lure the armies of the world to this area in Israel known as the Mount of Megiddo or Armageddon. From Antichrist's perspective, he will have a better chance of defeating his numerous enemies if he can contain them in a single location.

My predecessor, Dr. W. A. Criswell, told me once about being on an airplane seated next to the chief of staff at the Pentagon. At that time, Dr. Criswell was preaching on the subject of Armageddon, so he asked the chief of staff if he thought it was ever likely that foot soldiers would be outdated and replaced by modern weapons of warfare (the book of Revelation describes infantrymen and horses). The general answered, "Never. We will always need soldiers to push our enemies together. Atomic weapons and hydrogen bombs are of no use if the enemy is deployed over the face of a continent. The only way that an atomic bomb is useful is when we have a concentration of the enemy so you can drop it on them. But in order to push those enemies together we must have an army to compress them." So it will be at the final world battle known as Armageddon.

One other thought. Although Revelation 16:13–14 says that evil spirits will lure the world forces to Armageddon, God is the ultimate cause of their gathering. First Kings 22 describes how God used an evil spirit to tempt Ahab to wage war against the city of Ramoth-gilead and suffer defeat. God will again employ evil spirits to accomplish the same purpose at Armageddon.

Possibly, like me, you have had the opportunity of standing on the Mount of Megiddo, looking out on this spectacular plain that was the sight of many Old Testament battles such as Barak and the Canaanites and Gideon against the Midianites. The plain is fourteen miles wide and twenty miles long. Napoleon called it "the most natural battlefield in the whole earth." Yet, as large as the area is, it is obviously not large enough to contain the number of forces described here . . . and it doesn't need to. This final world conflict will be waged up and down the entire length of Israel:

"And the wine press was trodden outside the city, and blood came out from the wine press, up to the horses' bridles, for a distance of two hundred miles" (Revelation 14:20).

But it is while the world forces are waging war against one another that God releases His final judgment against the earth:

"Then the seventh angel poured out his bowl upon the air, and a loud voice came out of the temple from the throne, saying, 'It is done'" (Revelation 16:17).

One factor that differentiates this judgment from the preceding ones described in the last chapter is that it will be released "upon the air" instead of on the earth. Could this be a description of some great nuclear explosion? The proliferation of nuclear weapons across the globe is certainly alarming. The Federation of American Scientists estimates that approximately seventeen thousand nuclear warheads currently exist.[2]

How powerful are these nuclear weapons?

A rudimentary nuclear bomb would have the destructive power equal to 1 kiloton (1000 tons) of high explosives. Had such a bomb been detonated by terrorists in the center of New York on September 11, 2001, the force would have been enough to level most of Manhattan, Brooklyn, and Staten Island, killing millions of people. Additionally, that one nuclear bomb detonated in central New York City would have destroyed the United Nations Headquarters, the major broadcast network centers, and the New York Stock Exchange, wreaking economic and social chaos in our country and around the globe.

One crudely made nuclear bomb with a kiloton of destructive power could level a city. However, one standard nuclear warhead on a US or British strident submarine has a force equal to 100 kilotons (100,000 tons) of explosive power. If one thousand of these more powerful nuclear warheads were deployed in a world conflict, it would be enough to destroy the human race through the direct and indirect effects (such as radiation poisoning and environmental pollution) of such a nuclear holocaust. Today, the United States has a nuclear arsenal equaling eighteen hundred megatons, which is enough to destroy humanity eighteen times and Russia possesses twenty-nine hundred megatons of destructive power, capable of obliterating the human race twenty-nine times.

With the current heightened hostilities in the Middle East, and given some of Israel's neighbors—particularly Iran—threatening to wipe Israel off the map, the world appears to be poised for some type of nuclear calamity.[3]

The following verses certainly indicate that something of the magnitude of a nuclear exchange marks the climax of the war of Armageddon:

> And there were flashes of lightning and sounds and peals of thunder; and there was a great earthquake, such as there had not been since man came to be upon the earth, so great an earthquake was it, and so mighty. The great city was split into three parts, and the cities of the nations fell. Babylon the great was remembered before God, to give her

the cup of the wine of His fierce wrath. And every island
fled away, and the mountains were not found. (Revelation
16:18–20)

But this catastrophic judgment against the earth is only a
prelude to the most dramatic event in human history—the return
of Jesus Christ.

HERE COMES THE KING!

After a brief interlude during which the apostle John gives further
details concerning Babylon, he returns to the climax of the battle of
Armageddon. As the world forces are battling Antichrist, suddenly
the heavens open and the armies drop their weapons as they stare
into the sky in stunned silence:

> And I saw heaven opened, and behold, a white horse,
> and He who sat upon it is called Faithful and True,
> and in righteousness He judges and wages war. . . . He
> is clothed with a robe dipped in blood, and His name
> is called The Word of God. And the armies which are
> in heaven, clothed in fine linen, white and clean, were
> following Him on white horses. From His mouth comes
> a sharp sword, so that with it He may strike down the
> nations, and He will rule them with a rod of iron; and
> He treads the wine press of the fierce wrath of God, the
> Almighty. (Revelation 19:11, 13–15)

It is obvious that the rider of the white horse is the Lord Jesus Christ. But who are the "armies which are in heaven"? That's you and I! How do I know that? Because earlier in Revelation 19, John described what is happening in heaven just prior to Christ's return to earth. Christians will be in heaven, preparing to return to earth with the Lord to enjoy the marriage supper of the Lamb, a celebration that will occur when Christ returns to establish His kingdom on the earth.

How do you dress for a wedding? As a pastor I have seen a few people come to a wedding dressed in blue jeans and a T-shirt, but most people prefer something a little more formal. As believers prepare for the wedding supper with Jesus Christ, we too will dress in our best:

"'The marriage of the Lamb has come and His bride has made herself ready.' It was given to her to clothe herself in fine linen, bright and clean; for the fine linen is the righteous acts of the saints" (Revelation 19:7–8).

When we return to earth with Christ for this celebration, we will not be wearing Brioni suits or Chanel dresses, but our garments will be related to the righteous deeds we have performed as believers. Before we trust in Christ as our Savior, our good works are worthless before God. The best we can do, Isaiah the prophet said, is like a filthy rag to God (Isaiah 64:6). We are only saved by God's grace. However, *after* we become a Christian, our good works are vitally important and will determine what kind of eternity we experience (we will discuss this further in chapter 9).

The armies that return to earth with Christ are described as being dressed "in fine linen, white and clean" (Revelation 19:14) which clearly identifies them as those of us who are already in heaven. The world forces that were understandably startled by the appearance of Christ and His followers descending from heaven will regain their composure and actually unite to fight Christ and His army:

"And I saw the beast and the kings of the earth and their armies assembled to make war against Him who sat on the horse and against His army" (Revelation 19:19).

In the past I have heard some preachers and teachers describe Christians as some type of heavenly medieval knights, charging forward on horseback as they flail their swords and slaughter the forces of Satan. Such a scene might appeal to testosterone-charged men, but most women wince at such a thought. And people like me who have only ridden a horse twice (and fallen off both times) are more than a little concerned about handling a horse *and* a sword at the same time.

If you share those concerns, don't worry. Contrary to such popular descriptions, the Lord will not need our assistance in winning this battle. He is able to defeat these armies of the world without lifting a finger:

From His mouth comes a sharp sword, so that with it He may strike down the nations, and He will rule them with a rod of iron; and He treads the wine press of the fierce wrath of God, the Almighty. . . . And the rest were killed with the sword which came from the mouth of Him who sat on the horse, and all the birds were filled with their flesh. (Revelation 19:15, 21)

Just as God destroyed an army of 185,000 Assyrians in an instant (see 2 Kings 19:35), the same God will slay the armies of the earth with the sharp sword of His Word.

ONE OR TWO COMINGS?

Before we look at the three distinct purposes for Christ's visible return to earth, it might be helpful to explain both the similarities and the differences between the Rapture of the Church (described in chapter 4) and the Second Coming of Jesus Christ, prophesied throughout the Old Testament and described in Revelation 19. Those who believe in a Posttribulation Rapture (see chapter 4) view the Rapture and the Second Coming of Christ as practically a single event, occurring toward the end of the Tribulation. But those who advocate a Pretribulation Rapture of the Church believe that the Rapture and the Second Coming are two distinct events, separated by the seven years of Tribulation.

One reason that Posttribulationists and others believe that the Rapture and the Second Coming are synonymous is because the Bible uses the same words to describe both events:

- *parousia* (which means "coming," "arrival," or "presence" and is found in 1 Thessalonians 4:15 and Matthew 24:27);

- *apokalupsis* (which means "unveiling" or "revelation" and is used in 1 Corinthians 1:7 and 2 Thessalonians 1:7);
- *epiphaneia* (which means "manifestation" and is used in 2 Timothy 4:8 and 2 Thessalonians 2:8).[4]

Each of these words is used to describe both the Rapture and Second Coming of Christ. So isn't it natural to assume that these are both the same events?

In chapter 4 we saw that things can have common elements yet still be quite different. Both my wife and my two daughters possess eyes, ears, noses, the same coloring, and warm personalities. They are similar in many ways, but no one would argue they are the same people. The same truth applies to the Rapture and the Second Coming of Christ. In both events there will be a coming of the Lord from heaven (*paraousia*), a revealing of His glory as the Son of God (*apokalupsis*), and a visible manifestation of Himself (*epiphaneia*).

But there are also some major differences between the Rapture and the Second Coming that deserve our attention. First, many prophecies must be fulfilled prior to the Second Coming of Christ including the return of Israel to her homeland, the rebuilding of the temple, and the events of the Great Tribulation described in Revelation 6–19. However, *no* prophecies must be fulfilled before the Rapture of the Church occurs. At any moment, the trumpet could sound and believers could be caught up to meet the Lord in the air. That is why we say that the Rapture is "imminent"—it could happen at any moment. Since many of the prophecies concerning the Second Coming have already been fulfilled (such as

Israel returning to her homeland), the Rapture, which occurs seven years earlier, is closer than ever before.

Another difference between the Rapture and the Second Coming involves the Lord's final destination. At the Rapture, Christ's feet never touch the earth. Instead, He appears "in the air" (1 Thessalonians 4:17) to meet believers. But at the Second Coming, the Lord's feet will touch the earth, and when they do, what a topological reaction there will be! Recently I stood on the Mount of Olives and read to our tour group this verse, which describes what will happen at the Second Coming:

> In that day His feet will stand on the Mount of Olives, which is in front of Jerusalem on the east; and the Mount of Olives will be split in its middle from east to west by a very large valley, so that half of the mountain will move toward the north and the other half toward the south. (Zechariah 14:4)

Third, after the Rapture, Jesus returns to heaven with His believers. But at the Second Coming, Jesus returns to earth with believers to establish His kingdom.

Fourth, the Rapture is a mystery that is never mentioned in the Old Testament and only involves the Church. But the Second Coming is predicted many times in the Old Testament since it involves God's program for Israel, the Church, and the world.

Fifth, after the Rapture, only believers will be judged at the "bema" judgment (we will discuss this judgment in chapter 9).

The result of the judgment determines rewards in heaven. After the Second Coming, Israel and Gentile nations will be judged. The result of their judgment determines their eternal destiny.

Sixth, after the Rapture there is no physical change in the earth. But after the Second Coming, part of the curse against the earth is removed, and the planet will enjoy a partial renovation (a phenomenon we will explore further in the next chapter).

Seventh, after the Rapture, Satan runs rampant on the earth for seven years. After the Second Coming, Satan is bound for one thousand years.

Eighth, the Rapture occurs instantaneously ("in the twinkling of an eye," as 1 Corinthians 15:52 says), but the Second Coming is the climax of a worldwide conflict involving millions of people.

Finally, at the Rapture only believers will see the Lord Jesus Christ. But at the Second Coming unbelievers will "look on [Him] whom they have pierced" (Zechariah 12:10) and "every knee will bow . . . and . . . every tongue will confess that Jesus Christ is Lord, to the glory of God the Father" (Philippians 2:10–11).

Why a Second Coming?

Why is a literal, physical return of Jesus Christ to the earth really important?

When my wife and I were in high school, she attended a liberal church whose pastor denounced the basic tenets of the Christian faith: the deity of Christ, the substitutionary death of Christ for our sins, the existence of heaven and hell, and the literal and visible

Second Coming of Christ. One Easter Sunday morning I was driving down the highway in my blue Volkswagen Bug on the way to the church I now pastor in downtown Dallas. That morning Billy Graham was scheduled to speak to our congregation. His topic? "The Second Coming of Jesus Christ." As I eagerly anticipated his message, I thought I would turn on the radio and listen to the sermon my future wife was hearing in her church. Coincidentally, her pastor was also preaching on the Second Coming, but with quite a different twist. I will never forget what I heard him say.

> For two thousand years people have believed that Jesus Christ is coming back to earth to set up some kingdom. And yet, He hasn't come. And He *isn't* coming either. The first time Jesus came to earth was at Bethlehem. But His Second Coming is when He comes into your heart.

This pastor's words were almost identical to warning of the apostle Peter, who described the taunting by unbelievers in the last days:

> Know this first of all, that in the last days mockers will come with their mocking, following after their own lusts, and saying, "Where is the promise of His coming? For ever since the fathers fell asleep, all continues just as it was from the beginning of creation" . . . But do not let this one fact escape your notice, beloved, that with the Lord one day is like a thousand years, and a thousand years like

one day. The Lord is not slow about His promise, as some count slowness, but is patient toward you, not wishing for any to perish but for all to come to repentance. (2 Peter 3:3–4, 8–9)

The Lord *is* returning to earth for a least three important purposes. First, He is coming to complete the prophecies of the Bible. There are hundreds of prophecies in both the Old and New Testaments concerning the Lord's return to earth that demand fulfillment. If those prophecies are not fulfilled, then the trustworthiness of all of God's Word is suspect.

Second, Christ is coming to judge unbelievers. Again, both the Old and New Testaments promise that one day the Lord is going to judge the ungodly:

And He will strike the earth with the rod of His mouth,
And with the breath of His lips He will slay the wicked. (Isaiah 11:4)

But by His word the present heavens and earth are being reserved for fire, kept for the day of judgment and destruction of ungodly men. (2 Peter 3:7)

Although a number of unbelievers will be killed during the Great Tribulation, many of them will survive and must be judged by Christ before He begins His rule upon the earth (to be discussed further in the next chapter).

Finally, Christ is coming to reclaim the earth, which was lost to Satan. If believers are simply caught up in the air to live with Christ in heaven forever, then Satan has been successful in usurping God's creation. Do you believe that God is going to say, "Satan, you've won. You can have the earth, and I'll take heaven. You stay in your corner of the universe, and I'll stay in mine"? Not on your life!

A seminary student was leaving the school gymnasium after a game of basketball with several friends. As he left, he was surprised to discover a janitor sitting in the bleachers reading the book of Revelation. Thinking of his own study of the book in a New Testament class, he asked the uneducated janitor in a somewhat condescending tone if he understood that complex book of the Bible. "Oh yes, I understand it. It means that Jesus is gonna win."[5]

The literal and visible return of Jesus Christ to earth means that Jesus is going to reclaim what is rightfully His. Jesus is going to win ... and so are we!

Chapter Seven

||||||||||||||||||||||||||||||||||||||||||||||||||

HEAVEN ON EARTH

Years ago a mother wrote a letter to an advice columnist in a newspaper questioning the goodness of God. The woman's beautiful twenty-two-year-old daughter had been killed by a drunk driver. The mother got on her knees and pleaded with God to bring her daughter back to life. "You can do anything. You can perform miracles. . . . Please God, let me trade places with her—please let me lie in that coffin, and let her out to live her life." God refused to honor her request. At times, the mother confesses, she had thought of suicide but lacked the "courage" to pull the trigger or take the pill that would end her relentless pain. Meanwhile, the drunk driver who killed the girl spent less than six months behind bars. "Today, he walks in the sun while my little girl is in a dark grave."

The mother closed her letter by saying, "God didn't answer my prayers, and I resent being told that I have no right to question God. If there is a God, and if I ever get to meet Him face to face, you can bet your life I will have plenty of whys for him to answer.

I want to know why my little girl died and that drunk was allowed to go on living. I love her more than my life, and I miss her so. I am mad that I am having to live in a world where she no longer lives. I want to know why. . . . I don't fear the Lord. And I don't fear hell, either. I know what hell is like. I've already been there since the day my precious daughter was killed."[1]

Although we might wince at that mother's defiant attitude toward her Creator, we can empathize with her questions. If there is a God, why does He allow murderers to run free, babies to be sexually abused, and hundreds of millions around the globe to starve to death? Why doesn't He create a world that is free from injustice, conflict, suffering, and death?

We know from Genesis 1–2 that such a world once existed, until sin caused that paradise to be lost to Satan's control. But it has not been lost forever. The most prominent prophetic promise in the Bible is that one day Jesus Christ is going to return to earth and establish a world order that is characterized by perfect peace, justice, and freedom from suffering. That period in history is called the Millennium, and it is the focus of this chapter.

THE MILLENNIUM IN PERSPECTIVE

Next to the Rapture, the Millennium is the most hotly debated aspect of Bible prophecy. You have probably heard the terms *premillennial*, *postmillennial*, and *amillennial* (terms we will later explain in detail) and wondered what all the fuss is about. The question is simple, but crucial: "Is Jesus Christ going to return to earth and establish His kingdom on earth?" How you answer that question not only affects your understanding of the future, but it also impacts how you interpret many of the prophecies concerning the kingdom of God found in the Old and New Testament.

The word *millennium* comes from the Latin words *milli*, meaning "thousand," and *annum*, meaning "year." Although the word "millennium" is not found in Scripture, the concept is clearly taught throughout the Bible, including Revelation 20.

Let's first set the scene for Revelation 20. We are at the end of the seven year period known as the Tribulation. The climax of the Tribulation is the battle/war known as Armageddon in which the world forces battle against the great dictator known as Antichrist. In the midst of that battle the heavens suddenly part, and Christ returns to earth with His followers. John describes the fate of Antichrist and his assistant known as the false prophet:

> And the beast was seized, and with him the false prophet who performed the signs in his presence, by which he deceived those who had received the mark of the beast and those who worshipped his image; these two were thrown alive into the lake of fire which burns with brimstone. (Revelation 19:20)

But what about the power behind Antichrist and the false prophet? What happens to Satan when Christ returns? John answers that question beginning in chapter 20:

Then I saw an angel coming down from heaven, holding the key of the abyss and a great chain in his hand. And he laid hold of the dragon, the serpent of old, who is the devil and Satan, and bound him for a *thousand years;* and he threw him into the abyss, and shut it and sealed it over him, so that he would not deceive the nations any longer, until the *thousand years* were completed; after these things he must be released for a short time.

Then I saw thrones, and they sat upon them, and judgment was given to them. And I saw the souls of those who had been beheaded because of their testimony of Jesus and because of the word of God, and those who had not worshiped the beast or his image, and had not received the mark on their forehead and on their hand; and they came to life and reigned with Christ for a *thousand years.* The rest of the dead did not come to life until the *thousand years* were completed. This is the first resurrection. Blessed and holy is the one who has a part in the first resurrection; over these the second death has no power, but they will be priests of God and of Christ and will reign with him for a *thousand years.* (Revelation 20:1–6; emphasis mine)

Later we will look at some of the characteristics of the Millennium that John mentions in this passage, but for now I want you to notice the repetition of phrase "thousand years" in this paragraph. It is found not just once or twice, but five times in six verses! Why is that significant?

Suppose you were to send a letter to your brother saying, "The day after Christmas I would like to come and stay at your house for thirteen days. For thirteen days I will enjoy visiting with you and your family. If thirteen days is too long, please let me know." You arrive at your brother's house the day after Christmas, just as you promised. You enjoy several delightful days together. However, on the third day, your brother informs you that he is leaving on a ski trip for two weeks.

"I thought you understood that I would be staying with you for thirteen days."

"I am so sorry," he replies. "I didn't think you actually *meant* thirteen days; I thought you were speaking figuratively."

Figuratively? How could you have been more clear? You didn't say you were going to stay "for a while" or "until after the first of the year." You were very specific—thirteen days. I wonder if the Lord doesn't experience some of that frustration when He hears well-meaning Christians trying to interpret Revelation 20:

- "I wonder how long Christ is really going to rule on the earth."
- "I wonder what John means by 'the earth.'"
- "I wonder if the binding of Satan should be taken figuratively or literally."

Assume for just a moment that Jesus Christ is going to return to earth and rule over the earth for one thousand years. How would John communicate that truth? He would use the very same words we find in Revelation 20. A thousand years means a thousand years. The earth means the earth. As someone wisely suggested about interpreting the Bible, "When the plain sense makes good sense, seek no other sense."

"Pre," "Post," or "A"?

Throughout history Christians have held various views concerning the nature and the timing of the Millennium. Specifically, the question is "When is the Second Coming of Christ in relation to the Millennium?"

The premillennial position (the view espoused in this book) is that the Second Coming of Christ occurs prior to ("pre") the Millennium. But the premillennial position is more than a question of timing. Premillennialists believe in a literal fulfillment of the Abrahamic Covenant we examined in chapter 2. Specifically, they believe that, one day, believing Israel—composed of those Israelites who trust in Christ for their salvation—is going to inhabit all of the land promised to Abraham, that Jesus Christ is going to rule from the throne of David in the city of Jerusalem, and that Satan will be restrained from any activity for one thousand years.

Premillennialists also see a distinction between the Church (believers saved between Pentecost and the Rapture) and Israel. Although there are benefits from the Abrahamic Covenant that will extend to the Church during the Millennium, there are other benefits that are peculiar to believing Israel. Since God made an unconditional promise to Abraham and his believing descendants, God is obligated to keep those promises. The Millennium will be that period in history when God will fulfill His promises to believing Israel.

Although some people have tried to distinguish between "historic premillennialism" and what is sometimes called "dispensational premillennialism," the reader should understand that such distinctions are dubious at best. Popular teacher and author Dr. Charles Ryrie writes,

> Opponents of the premillennial system have attempted to obscure the main issues involved by inventing distinctions between historic premillennialists, pretribulationalists, dispensationalists, and ultra-dispensationalists. Such distinctions are not warranted since the differences involved are so minor and since the roots of premillennialism go far deeper.[2]

Postmillennialists believe that Christ will return after ("post") the Millennium. Proponents of this view believe that the entire world will be evangelized, bringing about the peace and righteousness that will characterize the Kingdom Age. Postmillennialism thrived from the seventeenth century until the middle of the twentieth century. However, two world wars nearly extinguished this belief that the planet was going to get better and better until Christ returned.

Although classical postmillennialism is just about dead, there is a variation of it known as "reconstructionism" that is very popular today. Christian reconstructionists advocate believers using the political process to bring about the "kingdom of God" here on earth. If we can elect the right individuals into office and legislate Christian reforms, then we can experience the kingdom rule of Christ, the reconstructionist believes. In my book *Twilight's Last Gleaming*, I explain that as Christians we do have the responsibility to act as "salt" and "light" in our society, just as Jesus commanded in Matthew 5:13–14. In Jesus' day, salt was a preservative that gave meat a longer shelf life in prerefrigeration times. Salt could not prevent the decay of meat; it simply delayed the decay. Eventually, the meat spoiled and had to be thrown out.

Similarly, Jesus is saying that, by acting as "salt," Christians have both the ability and the responsibility to delay the decay of our world. Electing godly leaders to office, upholding the sanctity of life and marriage, and pushing back against the immorality that is engulfing our culture is not going to prevent the ultimate collapse of our society and world, but it can delay it so that Christians have longer to serve as "light"—pointing people to Jesus Christ in this darkening world. To be clear, such actions are not going to "Christianize" our nation or world before the return of Christ. We cannot legislate the Millennium into existence. We are simply trying to prevent the premature deterioration our world in order to give more people an opportunity to trust in Jesus Christ.

The real debate in eschatology (the study of the end times) is between premillennialism and amillennialism. The word *amillennial* means "no millennium." Now, I must confess to you (if you haven't already figured this out by reading my biographical sketch on the back cover) that I come from a strong premillennial background. Between sitting under the preaching of my predecessor at First Baptist Dallas, Dr. W.A. Criswell, for thirty years and attending Dallas Theological Seminary for four years, I didn't have a chance! But in their zeal to defend the premillennial belief system, I have heard some premillennialists level some unfair charges against amillennialists: "Those infidels don't even believe the Bible. How can they not believe in a Millennium when it is so clearly taught in the Bible?"

The truth is that amillennialists *do* believe in a Millennium—of sorts. But the Millennium they describe is not physical, but spiritual; it is not earthly, but heavenly. Amillennialists interpret the thousand-year reign of Christ described in Revelation 20 as descriptive of Christ's rule in the hearts of His followers that began after the resurrection and will extend until the Second Coming. At that time, Christ will return to earth, judge the wicked, reward the righteous, and we will enter into eternity. Amillennialists claim that although God did make certain promises to Israel in the Old Testament, the Israelites forfeited those unfulfilled promises when they rejected Christ. The promises that were intended for Israel are now reserved for the Church. Furthermore, these promises have been transformed from the physical to the spiritual. Thus, the hope of Israel one day inheriting the Promised Land has now been transformed into the Church inheriting heaven.

What about the description in Revelation 20 of the binding of Satan for one thousand years? Amillennialists claim that Jesus Christ has already bound the power of Satan through several actions: (1) resisting him in the wilderness, (2) paying for man's sins at the cross, and (3) destroying the power of death at the resurrection. Thus, Christians are experiencing the Millennium now to the extent that they allow Christ to rule in their hearts according to the amillennial perspective.

I must admit that there is one aspect of amillennialism that is appealing to me: its simplicity! You don't need complicated charts to explain the end times from the amillennial viewpoint. The final events are simple: Church Age, Second Coming, judgments, and eternity. No separate Rapture, no complicated judgments, and no distinction between Israel and the Church.

Some years ago I assisted our denomination in writing Sunday school curriculum on Revelation. I was designated as the premillennial representative and another person served as the amillennial representative. We were scheduled to meet for two days and explain each chapter of Revelation from our particular viewpoints. I spent days preparing my material and arrived with charts, papers, and several stacks of books. My amillennial colleague strolled into the room with nothing except a pocket-sized New Testament! Our discussion leader would ask, "Robert, what is the premillennial view of the seven seals in Revelation 6?" I would launch into a detailed explanation while everyone's eyes glazed over. My amillennial friend would answer, "Probably symbolic." And so it went through most of the two days. In fact, I was so exhausted by the end of our seminar, I was about ready to convert to amillennialism myself. It is so much easier! But simplicity is not always synonymous with accuracy. Sometimes truth is complex.

Although amillennialism has been a popular millennial view throughout church history, I believe it has some serious problems, chief of which is the Abrahamic Covenant (see chapter 2). God's covenant with Abraham and his descendants was an unconditional promise, not based on Israel's faithfulness, but on the faithfulness of God. Although Israel would certainly suffer for her rebellion against God, He promised never to abandon His covenant with her. Remember Psalm 89?

If his sons forsake My law
And do not walk in My judgments,
If they violate My statutes
And do not keep My commandments,
Then I will punish their transgression with the rod
And their iniquity with stripes.
But I will not break off My lovingkindness from him,
Nor deal falsely in My faithfulness.
My covenant I will not violate,
Nor will I alter the utterance of My lips.
Once I have sworn by My holiness;
I will not lie to David.
His descendants shall endure forever
And his throne as the sun before Me.
(Psalm 89:30–36)

The unconditional nature of the Abrahamic Covenant is the main reason that I believe that Christians can look forward to a coming kingdom of Christ on this earth. Such a kingdom was prophesied in the Old Testament, anticipated in the Gospels and Epistles, and fulfilled in Revelation.

OLD TESTAMENT PROPHECIES OF THE KINGDOM

Just about every Old Testament prophet looked forward to the coming kingdom of God on earth. Just consider some of these prophecies:

And He will judge between the nations,
And will render decisions for many peoples;
And they will hammer their swords into plowshares
and their spears into pruning hooks.
Nation will not lift up sword against nation,
And never again will they learn war. (Isaiah 2:4)

"Behold, the days are coming," declares the LORD,
"When I will raise up for David a righteous Branch;
And He will reign as king and act wisely
And do justice and righteousness in the land.
In His days Judah will be saved,
And Israel will dwell securely;
And this is His name by which He will be called,
'The LORD our righteousness.'"
(Jeremiah 23:5–6)

"But this is the covenant which I will make with the house of Israel after those days," declares the LORD, "I will put My law within them, and on their heart I will write it; and I will be their God, and they shall be My people. They will not teach again, each man his neighbor and each man his brother, saying, 'Know the LORD,' for they will all know Me, from the least of them to the greatest of them," declares the LORD, "for I will forgive their iniquity, and their sin I will remember no more." (Jeremiah 31:33–34)

"Sing for joy and be glad, O daughter of Zion; for behold I am coming and I will dwell in your midst," declares the Lord. "Many nations will join themselves to the Lord in that day and will become My people. Then I will dwell in your midst, and you will know that the Lord of hosts has sent Me to you. The Lord will possess Judah as His portion in the holy land, and will again choose Jerusalem." (Zechariah 2:10–12)

Some would say that these prophecies were fulfilled when the Jews returned to Palestine (beginning in 538 BC) after seventy years of Babylonian captivity. However, there are aspects of these promises that were left unfulfilled. For example, the Israelites did not dwell in the land in safety after their return and were eventually dispersed from the land by the Romans in AD 70. Furthermore, one can hardly say that there was any extended spiritual revival in the land when they returned, as Jeremiah anticipated. Everyone did *not* "know the Lord." Instead, the Israelites quickly fell into apostasy.

Acknowledging these problems, others have wanted to point to heaven as the ultimate fulfillment of these Old Testament prophecies. But there are difficulties with that interpretation as well. Let's look again at one of the best-known verses regarding the coming kingdom of God:

I will also rejoice in Jerusalem and be glad in My people;
And there will no longer be heard in her
The voice of weeping and the sound of crying.

No longer will there be in it an infant who lives but a
   few days,
Or an old man who does not live out his days;
For the youth will die at the age of one hundred And the
   one who does not reach the age of one hundred
Will be thought accursed.
They will build houses and inhabit them;
They will also plant vineyards and eat their fruit.
   (Isaiah 65:19–21)

As we saw in chapter 1, this verse is obviously not referring to life on the earth as we know it today. When the Jews returned from Babylon to Jerusalem, babies still died and few men lived for a century. However, this verse cannot refer to heaven, either, since the Bible clearly says there will be no death in heaven. The Old Testament prophets were not describing the earth as it is or heaven as it will be. Instead, they were anticipating a period in which believers will experience the best of both worlds: heaven on earth!

NEW TESTAMENT PROPHECIES OF THE KINGDOM

When Christ came to earth the first time, He offered to establish His kingdom on earth. He announced, "Repent, for the kingdom of heaven is at hand" (Matthew 4:17). Jesus instructed His disciples to proclaim the coming of His kingdom: "And as you go, preach, saying, 'The kingdom of heaven is at hand'" (Matthew

10:7). Had the Jews received Christ as the Messiah, I believe He would have established His rule over the earth at that moment.

But what about the cross? If Christ had been installed as king of the Jews, there would have been no crucifixion. And if there had been no crucifixion, there would be no salvation. Obviously, God knew all along that Israel would reject Christ. And as the apostle Paul explained, God used Israel's rejection to accomplish His ultimate plan. Nevertheless, Christ's offer of a kingdom was legitimate.

But when Israel rejected Christ as Messiah (a rejection that occurred progressively throughout Christ's three-year ministry on earth and culminated with His crucifixion), Christ's kingdom on earth was not forfeited, but simply postponed.

It might be helpful here to clearly define what the phrase "kingdom of God" or "kingdom of heaven" means. A monarch's kingdom consists of the territory he rules. So, the "kingdom of God" refers to that place where God's rule is complete and uncontested. While it's true that God is ultimately sovereign over all His creation, He has chosen to allow a rebellion against His will in one small part of the universe.

However, that condition is only temporary. During the Millennium, God's authority will be universally recognized and obeyed, and the entire world will experience the benefits of submitting to God's rule. Think about it. Wouldn't much of the heartache and suffering in the world be alleviated if everyone simply obeyed God's commands? Imagine a world in which there were no more murders, no adultery and divorce, no addictive behavior, and everyone loved others as much as they loved themselves. That will be the kind of world everyone will enjoy under the kingdom rule of Christ called the Millennium.

However, Christians don't have to wait until then to experience the dividends of submitting to God's rule over our lives. In Matthew 13 Jesus told a series of stories illustrating how God's kingdom operates right now in the hearts of those who choose to submit themselves to God's rule. Right now you can enjoy "kingdom benefits" such as freedom from worry, harmony in relationships, power over addictions, and content with your financial resources by recognizing God's right to rule over your life.

Nevertheless, the fact that "the kingdom of God" should operate in the lives of Christians right now does not negate a future time when the kingdom of God will extend over the entire planet. The apostles clearly expected such a kingdom, as evidenced by their question to Jesus before He ascended into heaven: "Lord, is it at this time You are restoring the kingdom to Israel?"

Let's pause here and consider that question and some possible answers Jesus could have offered.

Suppose for the last several weeks I had been promising my wife, Amy, "One day soon I'm going to fix the leaky faucet in the bathroom." Several days before I leave for an out-of-town speaking engagement, Amy asks, "Robert, are you going to repair the faucet before you leave?" It would be a natural question. Since I am about to depart, Amy is anxious for me to make good on my promise so that she is not left to endure an irritating drip. (I'm referring to water, not myself.)

Jesus had promised His disciples that He was going to engage in some repair work Himself. By fulfilling the hope of the Old Testament prophets and establishing His kingdom on earth, Jesus would fix the injustices and inequities His disciples and all the world's population were enduring. The coming kingdom of Christ was such a prominent feature in Jesus' teaching that the disciples naturally wanted to know when this great event would occur.

Imagine for a moment that the disciples had completely misinterpreted Christ's teachings about the Millennium. Suppose that there was not going to be a literal, physical reign of Christ from Jerusalem. Instead, the rule of Christ had already begun in the hearts the disciples, as the amillennialists claim. Wouldn't this have been a perfect time for Christ to clear up the misunderstanding? Jesus could have easily responded to the apostles' question about the kingdom by saying, "Guys, you have got this thing all wrong. Israel is *never* going to have the kingdom restored to her. She forfeited those rights when she rejected Me. The kingdom I am offering is spiritual, not physical."

But Jesus never denied that He would one day establish His kingdom on earth. Instead, He said, "It is not for you to know times or epochs which the Father has fixed by His own authority" (Acts 1:7). The disciples did not misunderstand the nature of the coming kingdom, but simply the timing of it. Christ would return to establish His kingdom according to God's timetable, not theirs.

Thus, when we come to the Revelation, we finally see the kingdom of Christ established on the earth. Listen to the announcement of the angel when Christ returns to earth:

Then the seventh angel sounded; and there were loud voices in heaven, saying, "The kingdom of the world has become the kingdom of our Lord and of His Christ; and He will reign forever and ever." (Revelation 11:15)

This declaration signals the beginning of Christ's physical rule on the earth—a rule prophesied by the prophets, anticipated by the apostles, and fulfilled by Christ.

FOUR THINGS EVERY CHRISTIAN SHOULD KNOW ABOUT THE MILLENNIUM

Up to this point we have defined the Millennium, examined differing views of the Millennium, and established the scriptural basis for the Millennium in both the Old and New Testaments. But what is life in the Millennium actually going to be like for those of us who are believers? If all of this discussion about the Millennium has seemed a little academic, allow me to suggest four aspects of this thousand-year period of time that should be of interest to you.

1. Only Christians will enter into the Millennium.

The coming kingdom of Christ is reserved for Christians only. Although a number of people will be killed during the Great Tribulation, many others will survive. Some of those survivors will be Christians, others will be unbelievers. When Christ returns to earth, His first order of business will be to preside over a series of judgments described in Matthew 25. Those who survive the judgments will be welcomed into the Millennium; those who don't will be cast into the eternal lake of fire. Look at what Jesus had to say about those judgments:

> But when the Son of Man comes in His glory, and all the angels with Him, then He will sit on His glorious throne. All the nations will be gathered before Him; and He will separate them from one another, as the shepherd separates the sheep from the goats; and He will put the sheep on His right, and the goats on the left. Then the King will say to those on His right, "Come, you who are blessed of My Father, inherit the kingdom prepared for you from the foundation of the world . . . " Then He will also say to those on His left, "Depart from Me, accursed ones, into the eternal fire which has been prepared for the devil and his angels." (Matthew 25:31–34, 41)

Every Christian needs to understand that there are no second chances for salvation once Christ has returned. Only believers will enter into the Millennium.

2. Christians will rule with Christ in the Millennium.

Although Christ will be ruling the world from David's throne in Jerusalem, He will delegate some of His ruling authority to the twelve apostles (Matthew 19:28), to the Christians martyred during the Tribulation (Revelation 20:4), and to those of us who are Christians (2 Timothy 2:12). As we will see in chapter 9, our ruling responsibilities will be determined by our faithfulness to Christ in this life, as illustrated in the parable of the minas recorded in Luke 19:11–27.

A natural question is, "What (or whom) will we rule over in the Millennium?" Although the Bible is not completely clear about this, Scripture does indicate that we will assist Christ in ruling over cities, over other believers, and even over the angels! When the apostle Paul was trying to explain to the Corinthians why they should not sue one another in pagan courts and, instead, rely on wise Christians to settle disputes, he uses this rationale:

> Or do you not know that the saints will judge the world? If the world is judged by you, are you not competent to constitute the smallest law courts? Do you not know that we will judge angels? How much more matters of this life? (1 Corinthians 6:2–3)

In other words, we had better learn how to render good decisions in this life since in the next life we are going to be administering other people and even angels!

3. Jerusalem will be the center of the Millennial Kingdom.

Numerous Old Testament prophecies indicate that Jesus Christ will reign on earth from the city of Jerusalem (Isaiah 2:2–4; Micah

4:1–2; Zechariah 2:10–11). However, Jerusalem and all of Israel will undergo a tremendous topological transformation at the Second Coming of Christ that will result in greater fertility and productivity. This enlarged area will also accommodate the division of land among the twelve tribes of Israel described in Ezekiel 48 and the Millennial Temple detailed in Ezekiel 40–46.

The centrality of Jerusalem during the Millennium helps explain why Jerusalem will continue to be a hotbed of conflict and controversy until then. Although the Jews have maintained a presence in Israel for thirty-five hundred years and have been the majority residents of Jerusalem since 1852, many dispute Israel's claim that Jerusalem belongs to her.[3]

Recently, production of a European documentary film on Jerusalem was disrupted because Palestinian authorities claimed the film would present Jerusalem as a united city belonging to Israel. "This is not one city, it is two cities," says Dimitri Diliani, spokesman in East Jerusalem for the Fatah party of the Palestinian President Mahmoud Abbas. "The whole idea of accepting the occupiers' [Israel's] claims that this is one city is totally wrong. This has political ramifications," Diliani told Reuters.[4]

The unrelenting desire of Muslims to control a portion or all of Jerusalem is curious since the Qu'ran does not mention Jerusalem once, in contrast to the Bible which refers to Jerusalem 667 times in the Old Testament and 144 times in the New Testament. Nevertheless, the battle for control of Jerusalem is ground zero for the unending Israeli-Arab conflict today that will one day be the catalyst for the global conflict the Bible calls Armageddon.

4. Satan will be temporarily bound during the Millennium.

One reason for the peace, righteousness, prosperity, physical healing and longevity of life that will characterize the Millennium is that Satan will be imprisoned during these one thousand years. Look at how John describes this scene in Revelation 20:

> Then I saw an angel coming down from heaven, holding the key of the abyss and a great chain in his hand. And he laid hold of the dragon, the serpent of old, who is the devil and Satan, and bound him for a thousand years; and he threw him into the abyss, and shut it and sealed it over him, so that he would not deceive the nations any longer, until the thousand years were completed; after these things he must be released for a short time. (Revelation 20:1–3)

Who is it that is bound for one thousand years? Just so that no one misses it, John is as specific as he can be: "the dragon, the serpent of old, who is the devil and Satan." Since the beginning of recorded history, Satan has been deceiving nations and individuals into thinking they could live successfully apart from their Creator. But for the one thousand years of the Millennium, the deceiver will be bound, and the curse he brought into the world will be partially lifted. Although believers who are in their natural bodies during the Millennium will live longer than they do today, they will still die, as evidenced in Isaiah 65:20:

No longer will there be in it an infant who lives but a few days,
Or an old man who does not live out his days;
For the youth will die at the age of one hundred
And the one who does not reach the age of one hundred
Will be thought accursed.

I imagine an alarm bell just sounded in your mind. "Believers who are in their natural bodies? What in the world are you talking about, Robert?" Although only Christians will enter into the Millennium, some will enter in their natural bodies, while others will possess their supernatural bodies. Those believers who survive the Tribulation will enter into the Millennium in their natural bodies, while those of us who return with Christ will be in our supernatural bodies that we received at the Rapture. We will look at this unusual phenomenon more in the next chapter.

RENOVATION OR RE-CREATION?

One way to understand the difference between the earth during the Millenium and the "new heaven and a new earth" that believers will experience after the Millennium (Revelation 21–22) is to think of the words "renovate" and "re-create." When I first came as pastor of First Baptist Church in Dallas we decided to renovate our preschool and children's space with new carpet, paint, and some imaginative theming. Everyone was thrilled by the vast improvement. However, I also knew that this was only a "temporary fix" until we could accomplish our ultimate vision—the complete re-creation of our entire church campus that covered six blocks of downtown Dallas.

One Saturday morning, we imploded the entire campus (including the renovated children's area) with hundreds of pounds of dynamite, reducing the entire campus into a pile of rubble. After six months of removing the debris, we completely re-created all of our church, including building a brand-new state-of-the-art children's facility, designed by a former Disney Imagineer. While the renovated children's space was vastly superior to what had been there for decades, it was nothing compared to the re-created facility our families are now enjoying.

In the same way, Christians during the Millennium will be amazed at the improvement of the renovated earth under Christ's rule. Much of the heartache and suffering that are a part of our everyday existence will vanish. But that renovated earth will be nothing compared to the re-created heaven and earth that we will one day enjoy.

Chapter Eight

||||||||||||||||||||||||||||||||||||||||||||||

FINAL JUDGMENT

Warren Wiersbe tells the story about a frontier town where a horse bolted and ran away with a wagon carrying a small boy. Seeing the child in danger, a young man risked his life to stop the runaway wagon. The rescued boy grew up to be a ruthless outlaw and one day found himself standing before a judge, awaiting sentencing for a serious crime. The prisoner recognized the judge as the man who, years before, had saved his life, so he pled for mercy on the basis of that earlier experience. But the words from the judge silenced his plea. "Young man, on that day I was your savior; today, I am your judge, and I sentence you to be hanged." [1]

Two thousand years ago Jesus Christ came to earth as a Savior. He suffered a humiliating and excruciating death to pardon us from the consequences of our sin. The next time He comes, however, He will come as a Judge and will say to those who have rejected Him, "I never knew you; depart from Me, you who practice lawlessness" (Matthew 7:23). In this chapter we are going to examine Christ's coming judgment of unbelievers, an event commonly referred to as the Great White Throne Judgment.

THE TWO RESURRECTIONS

The beginning of Revelation 20 describes the binding of Satan for one thousand years while Christ reigns over a renovated earth. As we saw in the previous chapter, only Christians will enter into the Millennium. Some of the Christians who enter the Millennium will be those of us who return with Jesus Christ in our resurrected bodies we received at the Rapture (see chapter 4). But beginning in Revelation 20:4, John describes another group of Christians he saw reigning with Christ—those Christians who were martyred during the Great Tribulation:

> Then I saw thrones, and they sat on them, and judgment was given to them. And I saw the souls of those who had been beheaded because of their testimony of Jesus and because of the word of God, and those who had not worshipped the beast or his image, and had not received the mark on their forehead and on their hand; and they came to life and reigned with Christ for a thousand years. The rest of the dead did not come to life until the thousand years were completed. This is the first resurrection. Blessed and holy is the one who has a part in the first resurrection; over these the second death has no power. (Revelation 20:4–6)

This term "first resurrection" introduces us to an important key to understanding Bible prophecy: the two resurrections. The word "resurrection" is a translation of the Greek word *anastasis*, which is found more than forty times in the Bible. The word refers to the raising of a fallen body and is always used to describe a physical resurrection. We have already seen that when a Christian dies, his spirit goes immediately into the presence of Jesus Christ (2 Corinthians 5:8) while his body is placed in the grave awaiting resurrection.

Similarly, as we will see in chapter 10, when an unbeliever dies, his spirit goes to a place of torment, while his body is placed in the grave awaiting a resurrection to eternal judgment. The Bible treats these two resurrections separately: the first resurrection is for Christians and results in eternal life. The second resurrection is reserved for unbelievers and results in eternal death. That is why John writes, "Blessed and holy is the one who has a part in the first resurrection; over these the second death has no power" (Revelation 20:6). Let's take a moment and look at this first resurrection in more detail.

THE FIRST RESURRECTION

Those of you who are parents understand how carpools work. The driver stops at different houses, collects children, and finally deposits them at the intended destination. Obviously, not everyone gets into the car at the same time, but they are all part of the carpool and eventually arrive at the same location. I want you to keep that analogy in mind as we discuss "the first resurrection." Think of the "first resurrection" as a type of heavenly carpool. All Christians will not receive their resurrected bodies simultaneously. Instead, the Bible teaches that there are four stages (or "pick-up points") for the first resurrection—which is the raising and transformation of our old bodies into our new bodies (remember, our *spirits* go to be with God the instant we die).

Some Christians will receive their new bodies at the Rapture, some at the beginning of the Millennium, and some after the Millennium. But every Christian's body is ultimately "picked up" and transported into the presence of God.

The apostle Paul explains this concept of the "first resurrection" in 1 Corinthians 15, the great resurrection chapter of the Bible that could have been subtitled, "Everything You Ever Wanted to Know about the Resurrection but Were Afraid to Ask." Paul spends the first nineteen verses of this chapter using Old Testament prophecies, eyewitness accounts, theology, and logic to defend the truth of Christ's physical resurrection from the grave. While some of the Corinthian believers were willing to concede Christ's resurrection, they could not believe that they would share in that same experience. So beginning in verse 20, Paul demonstrates that Christ's resurrection was not some isolated event, but it was the beginning of an extraordinary process—the resurrection of *every* believer: "But now Christ has been raised from the dead, the first fruits of those who are asleep."

The term *first fruits* doesn't mean much to us, but Jews understood exactly what Paul had in mind. Before the Israelites would harvest an entire crop, they would bring a sample of that crop to the priests as an offering (Leviticus 23:10). That offering was called "first fruits." Obviously, that offering was not the entire harvest; it was only a small, representative portion of what was to come. Similarly, Christ's resurrection was simply a sample of an even larger resurrection that is yet to come.

Like some of you, I have stood in front of that empty garden tomb in Jerusalem where the single greatest event in human history occurred. In the early morning hours of that first Easter morning, an angel appeared to a startled band of Roman soldiers and rolled the mighty stone away. In an instant, the power of death was forever broken as Jesus Christ "was declared the Son of God with power by the resurrection from the dead" (Romans 1:4). But as miraculous as that event was, it was only the tip of the iceberg. One day all Christians are going to experience the same kind of resurrection: "For as in Adam all die, so also in Christ all will be made alive. But each in his own order" (1 Corinthians 15:22-23).

Every Christian is going to receive a brand-new body (bodies that we will discuss further in chapter 10), but everyone must wait his turn! The key word here is "order," which comes from the Greek word *tagma*. The word *tagma* is a military term that refers to "rank" or "order." Paul is describing a military parade passing by, with each corps falling into position at the proper time (for those who can't identify with the military, think of the carpool). The first resurrection is like a parade that began when Christ rose from dead.[2] Throughout history, different Christians fall into their place in the parade at their appointed times. Notice that in this passage, Paul mentions four "pick-up points" or places where the corps falls into place:

> For as in Adam all die, so also in Christ all will be made alive. But each in his own order: Christ the first fruits, after that those who are Christ's at His coming, then comes the end, when He hands over the kingdom to the God and Father, when He has abolished all rule and all authority and power. (1 Corinthians 15:22–24)

Perhaps this chart will help you understand the four stages of the "first resurrection" and contrast it with the "second resurrection."

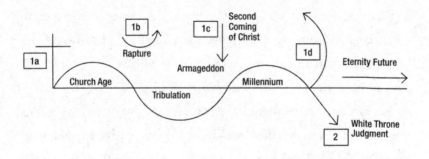

1a: "Christ the first fruits." Jesus Christ is the undisputed leader of this resurrection parade. In Ephesians 4:8 Paul again uses this word picture:

"When He ascended on high, He led captive a host of captives, And He gave gifts to men."

lb and lc: "After that, those who are Christ's at His coming." As we saw in chapter 4, the term *coming* refers to two events: the

Rapture and the Second Coming. Paul probably has both events in mind here. First Thessalonians 4:13–18 and 1 Corinthians 15:51–53 explain that at the Rapture, Christians who have died, as well as those believers who are alive at the time will receive their new bodies. But what about those believers who are killed during the Tribulation, as well as the Old Testament saints? They will receive their resurrection bodies at the Second Coming of Christ (seven years after the Rapture). Revelation 20:4 and Daniel 12:1–2 explain this truth.

1d: "then comes the end when He delivers up the kingdom." The fourth stage of "the first resurrection" will occur at the end of the Millennium when those Christians who survived the Tribulation and entered the Millennium in their natural bodies, as well as those who are born during the Millennium and choose to follow Christ, will receive their new bodies. (I will explain this further in the next section.)

THE SECOND RESURRECTION

"And the sea gave up the dead which were in it, and death and Hades gave up the dead which were in them" (Revelation 20:13). Unlike the first resurrection, the second resurrection is a single event that occurs at the end of the Millennium (the thousand-year reign of Christ on the earth) and will include all of the unsaved dead since the time of Adam.

The purpose of the first resurrection is that believers might receive their promised inheritance of a new body. Our new bodies will be identical to the resurrected body of Christ and, therefore, will be free from sin, suffering, and death.

The purpose of the second resurrection is that unbelievers might receive the punishment due them for their rejection of Christ. It is that final judgment of unbelievers that the apostle John describes in the last half of Revelation 20. But before that final judgment can occur, there is one last event that must transpire.

THE UNLEASHING OF SATAN

One night I was awakened by the chirping of a cricket. As I stealth-ily tiptoed into our bathroom, I noticed some movement in the planter box around the bathtub (we grow big crickets in Texas). Realizing that I had located the enemy, I jumped into the bathtub, pulled back the plastic plants and saw the creature running for its life. I quickly scooped him into my hand and started to deposit him in the watery grave of our toilet, when I was suddenly struck by compassion and let him go.

Do you believe that happened? Not on your life. When I finally captured that annoying insect, I wasn't about to release him. He had caused me too much trouble to ever merit a second chance . . . which is why I find Revelation 20:7 a little difficult to understand.

Remember that at the beginning of the Millennium the angel will lay hold of Satan and deposit him into the abyss. For the next one thousand years the whole earth enjoys a rest from most of the sin and suffering caused by the evil one. But then notice what happens:

When the thousand years are completed, Satan will be
released from his prison, and will come out to deceive the
nations which are in the four corners of the earth, Gog and
Magog, to gather them together for the war; the number of
them is like the sand of the seashore. And they came up on
the broad plain of the earth and surrounded the camp of
the saints and the beloved city, and fire came down from
heaven and devoured them. (Revelation 20:7–9)

At the end of the Millennium, God unleashes Satan from the
abyss and gives him one last opportunity to deceive the world. In
spite of the previous thousand years when Christ ruled the earth
with perfect righteousness, John says that a multitude of people will
choose to follow Satan and, as a result, will suffer God's judgment.

This raises a number of disturbing questions.

- Who are these people who choose to follow Satan in his final
  rebellion?
- Is it possible that genuine Christians could be deceived at the
  last moment and spend eternity in hell?
- Why does Revelation 20:3 say that God must release Satan
  "for a short time?"

First things first. Let's establish that it is impossible for a genuine
Christian to ever lose his salvation. Jesus said in John 10:28: "And I
give eternal life to them, and they will never perish; and no one will
snatch them out of My hand." Paul declared in Romans 11:29: "For

the gifts and the calling of God are irrevocable." Whoever these
people are who choose to follow Satan at the end of the Millennium,
they are not believers.

"But Robert, you said that only Christians enter the Millennium.
So how could these people who choose to follow Satan at the end of
the Millennium be anyone other than Christians?" This is where an
understanding of the different stages of the first resurrection helps us.

Remember that not all Christians receive their new bodies at
the same time. When Christ returns at the Second Coming to
establish His Millennial Kingdom, He will return with those of us
who received our new bodies at the Rapture. There will be another
group of people saved and martyred during the Tribulation who
will receive their new bodies at the Second Coming, prior to the
Millennium. But there is a final group of Christians who will enter
the Millennium in their natural bodies (see 1d on the chart). These
are people who were saved during Tribulation but not martyred.
This means that during the Millennium there will be Christians
who are in their resurrected bodies along with Christians who are
in their natural bodies.

I'll admit that this seems a little bizarre, but such an arrange-
ment answers a number of questions about the Millennium. For
example, how is it that people will be born and will die in the
Millennium as prophesied in Isaiah 65:20?

> No longer will there be in it an infant who lives but a few days,
> Or an old man who does not live out his days;
> For the youth will die at the age of one hundred

And the one who does not reach the age of one hundred
Will be thought accursed.

We know from Jesus' teaching in Luke 20:35–36 that Christians will not be able to procreate in their resurrected bodies. Furthermore, we know that our new bodies will never die (Revelation 21:4). Finally, we know that only Christians enter into the Millennium. Thus, the only explanation for birth and death in a Millennium populated only with Christians is that some Christians enter into this thousand-year period of time in their natural bodies. It is these Christians who produce children and who eventually die during the thousand-year reign of Christ. (Whether they receive their new bodies instantly or wait until the end of the Millennium is unclear.)

Such an explanation also answers the questions related to Satan's final rebellion at the conclusion of the Millennium. Those who choose to follow Satan will be some of these children born during the millennial reign of Christ. Although these children will be the offspring of genuine believers, they will have to make an individual choice to follow Christ. Such a choice is only possible if God releases Satan and provides them with an alternative. Amazingly, some of these who have enjoyed the Millennial blessings of Christ's rule over the earth will nevertheless succumb to Satan's deception and join his final rebellion against God. Their choice to follow Satan should forever lay to rest the myth that a perfect environment guarantees right behavior. Except for the Garden of Eden, the Millennium will be the most spiritually positive atmosphere mankind has ever experienced. Nevertheless, the sin nature that exists in every human heart will cause some to rebel against Christ.

After every person in every age has been given an opportunity to trust in Christ, God is now ready for the final judgment of mankind.

THE GREAT WHITE THRONE JUDGMENT

Contrary to what some people believe, there is not one final judgment that includes both believers and unbelievers. Instead, non-Christians are judged separately from Christians at a judgment commonly referred to as the Great White Throne Judgment, described in Revelation 20:11–15.

1. What happens at the Great White Throne Judgment?

Then I saw a great white throne and Him who sat upon it, from whose presence earth and heaven fled away, and no place was found for them. (Revelation 20:11)

After Satan's final rebellion, God will cast him into the lake of fire for an eternity of punishment (see Revelation 20:10). Apparently, God then destroys the present heaven and earth in preparation for the new heaven and earth (see 2 Peter 3:10–11; Revelation 20:11). Prior to the Great Tribulation, Revelation 4:2–5 pictures

God sitting on a throne surrounded by a rainbow, flashes of lightning, and other believers. But Revelation 20:11 describes a solitary throne suspended in space. This is obviously a different throne with a different Occupant. Jesus Christ is seated on this throne as He prepares to judge those who have rejected Him.

2. Who participates in the Great White Throne Judgment?

> And I saw the dead, the great and the small, standing before the throne . . . And the sea gave up the dead which were in it, and death and Hades gave up the dead which were in them; and they were judged, every one of them according to their deeds. (Revelation 20:13)

Some people want to simplify end-time events by insisting that there is only one final judgment for both believers and unbelievers. When Christ returns to earth, believers and unbelievers will stand before Christ to be commended or condemned. They believe that those who are commended will be welcomed into heaven; those who are condemned will be dispatched to hell.

But a careful study of the word translated "Hades" reveals that since the ascension of Christ this word is used to describe the abiding place of the unsaved dead (we will distinguish between "Hades" and "hell" in chapter 10). Thus, the only people involved in the Great White Throne Judgment are the unsaved dead who are presently occupying Hades.

3. What standard does Christ use at the Great White Throne Judgment?

By what standard will Christ judge the unbelievers who stand before Him at the White Throne Judgment? It may surprise you to learn that unbelievers will be judged by their works. Read carefully Revelation 20:12–13:

> And I saw the dead, the great and the small, standing before the throne, and books were opened; and another book was opened, which is the book of life; and the dead were judged from the things which were written in the books, *according to their deeds.* And the sea gave up the dead which were in it, and death and Hades gave up the dead which were in them; and they were judged, every one of them *according to their deeds.* (emphasis mine)

God keeps two sets of books on each of us. First, there is "the book of life," which contains the name of every believer who has trusted in Christ. Revelation 13:8 and Revelation 17:8 explain that the name of every believer was entered into this book before the foundation of the world. Is that because God *knew* beforehand who would trust in Christ or because He *determined* beforehand who would trust in Christ? Sorry, but we will have to save those answers for another book.

The point here is that those whose names are written in this book of life have nothing to fear, but those whose names do not appear in the book of life have *everything* to fear: "And if anyone's name was not found written in the book of life, he was thrown into the lake of fire" (Revelation 20:15).

But God also keeps a second set of books that record all of our deeds: the good, the bad, and the ugly. Every word, every thought, every action is carefully noted in our permanent record:

- The money you gave to United Way last year.
- The time you spent volunteering at hospice while in college.
- The effort you gave to organize a church outreach project.
- The lustful thought you had about your neighbor last week.
- The hateful words you said to your mate ten years ago.
- The income you failed to report on last year's tax return.

No good deed goes unnoted, and no sin goes unrecorded. It is all in "the books." Since God will not find the names of unbelievers written in the book of life, He opens this second set of books to judge unbelievers according to their works.

One of the saddest aspects to me about this whole judgment is the confidence many unbelievers will feel when this judgment begins. After the initial shock of standing before the Lord Jesus Christ, some unbelievers will breathe a sigh of relief when the Lord announces that they will be judged by their works. "By our works? This will be easy. I may not be perfect, but I'm no Osama Bin Laden either. I've loved my family, paid my taxes, and lived by the Golden Rule. Now, when do I get to check out those streets of gold I've heard about?" Ironically, it is the unbeliever's misplaced confidence in his own righteousness that has landed him before the Great White Throne.

The non-Christian's optimism suddenly turns to despair, however, when he realizes that the standard by which his life is judged is not his neighbor, but Jesus Christ Himself. One of the greatest misconceptions among non-Christians is that God grades on a curve: as long as we meet some minimum standards of decency, we can expect to be welcomed into heaven, they maintain. But Acts 17:31 tells us that the standard by which we will be judged will be the perfect life of Jesus Christ:

"He has fixed a day in which He will judge the world in righteousness through a Man whom He has appointed, having furnished proof to all men by raising Him from the dead."

At the Great White Throne Judgment every unbeliever will realize how far short he has fallen from the perfect righteousness of Jesus Christ.

4. What is the result of the Great White Throne Judgment?

What is the fate of those who are judged at the Great White Throne? Everyone who is resurrected for that judgment is cast into to the lake of fire:

Then death and Hades were thrown into the lake of fire. This is the second death, the lake of fire. And if anyone's name was not found written in the book of life, he was thrown into the lake of fire. (Revelation 20:14–15)

We are going to study this lake of fire in more detail in chapter 10. But notice that the lake of fire is a place of *eternal* suffering. We saw in Revelation 20:10 that Satan, the beast, and the false prophet were cast into this horrible place of punishment where they were "tormented day and night forever and ever." Imagine the worst pain you have ever experienced. As excruciating as that pain was, at least there was some relief that eventually came. But imagine experiencing that pain without any relief for millions, billions, and trillions of years. That is the horror that awaits those who are judged at the Great White Throne.

People frequently ask me, "How could a loving God ever sentence anyone to that kind of punishment?" The simple answer is that people choose to go to hell. Those participants in the Great White Throne judgment have said in effect, "I do not need Jesus Christ as my Savior. If God is going to judge me, I'll take my chances and let Him judge me by my works." Thus, God grants them their wish and judges them by their deeds.

The only way a holy God can allow any of us to enter heaven is by insisting that our righteousness equals that of His Son Jesus Christ. "That's impossible," you say, "I could never be as good as Jesus." Exactly! When I trust in Christ as my Savior, God takes the righteousness of His Son and wraps it around me. His righteousness becomes my righteousness.

My good friend Erwin Lutzer uses the following example to illustrate that truth. Imagine a book called *The Life and Times of Jesus Christ*. The book contains all the words, thoughts, and deeds of the only perfect Man who has ever lived. Now imagine another book titled *The Life and Times of [Your Name]*. This book is a record of everything you have ever done, said, or thought. Such a book reads like a supermarket tabloid. Now, picture God stripping both books of their covers. Then, He takes the cover of the book about Jesus' life, and he wraps it around the book of your life story. Next, God takes the cover of the book of your life story and wraps it around *The Life and Times of Jesus Christ*. When God opens the book with Jesus' name on the cover, He instead reads a book about your lies, corruption, and immorality. Jesus gets the blame for your sin.

But when God opens the book with your name on the cover, He reads a story about the perfection, purity, and complete obedience of His own Son. You get the credit for Jesus' perfect life.[3]

That is what the doctrine of justification is all about. God takes your sin and credits it to Jesus, and He takes Jesus' righteousness and credits it to your spiritual account. Paul explained the transaction this way: "[God] made [Jesus] who knew no sin to be sin on our behalf, so that we might become the righteousness of God in Him" (2 Corinthians 5:21).

As we close this very sobering chapter, let me ask you the most important question of all: What are you depending on to cause God to welcome you into heaven? Good works you have performed? Baptism? Church membership? A religious relative? Only those who understand their sinfulness and wrap themselves in the righteousness of Jesus Christ will escape the Great White Throne Judgment.

Each of us must choose the standard by which we want God to judge us: our righteousness or Christ's righteousness. It's one or the other. And it's a choice we must make before we die. If we wait until we find ourselves standing before Jesus Christ seated on that solitary white throne suspended in space, we have waited too long.

If you would like to receive the forgiveness that Christ offers you so that you can escape that final judgment and eternal sentence of suffering, may I suggest you pray this prayer to God:

> Dear God,
>
> I realize that I have fallen short of Your standards. I know that I have sinned in many ways and deserve to be punished by You. But I believe with all of my heart that You sent Jesus Christ to die for me. I believe that when Jesus hung on that cross, He took the punishment that I deserve. And now I am trusting in Jesus alone to save me from my sins. Thank You for forgiving me, and help me to live the rest of my life for You.
>
> In Jesus' name,
> Amen

If you prayed that prayer sincerely, you can know that not only will you escape the horror of hell, but you can also look forward to an event we will discuss in the next chapter.

Chapter Nine

||||||||||||||||||||||||||||||||||||||||||||||||

REWARDS IN HEAVEN

One of my mentors, the late Howard Hendricks, told the story about a downhill slalom racer who was greeted at the bottom of the course by his ski coach. "The good news is that you arrived at the finish marker faster than any of my other students. In fact, your time was the fastest ever on this course, perhaps even faster than the world record." But the coach wasn't finished. "The bad news is that you missed nearly every flag and are disqualified." To which the novice skier replied, "Flags? What flags?"

An expert skier understands that the route taken to get downhill is just as critical as reaching the goal. A good basketball player realizes that even more important than making a basket is making sure he is aiming toward the *right* basket.

Unfortunately, many Christians fail to understand a similar truth. Making it to heaven should not be the only goal of a believer. The Bible teaches that while all Christians will cross the "finish line," some will forfeit the loss of eternal rewards because their works have been disqualified by the Judge.[1] The result of such a loss will be severe disappointment and lasting regret.

"Wait a minute," some may protest. "Are you trying to tell me that it is possible that I could be disappointed in heaven?" Absolutely. One of the greatest myths about eternity is that all Christians will experience the same kind of heaven, and all unbelievers will experience the same kind of hell. Such a belief is illogical, and more importantly, unbiblical. In this chapter we are going to examine the reality of rewards in heaven.

FUTURE JUDGMENTS

In the last chapter we examined the judgment of all unbelievers known as the Great White Throne Judgment. Occurring at the end of the Millennium, this judgment is reserved for those who have refused to trust in Christ as Savior. Because they have rejected God's grace, they are judged by their works. The result of the judgment will be that every unbeliever will be cast into the lake of fire. Why? Because the unbeliever's deeds, as good as they may be, will fail to measure up to the perfection required by God.

Although the Great White Throne Judgment is the *final* judgment of unbelievers, it is not the *only* judgment of unbelievers. Matthew 25:31–46 teaches that when Christ returns to earth prior to the beginning of His Millennial Kingdom, He will judge the survivors of the Tribulation period. Although a large portion of the world's population will be destroyed during the Tribulation, many will escape death. Since only believers will be welcomed into the Millennium, it will be necessary for Christ to deal with the surviving unbelievers. While some Bible scholars see a whole series of judgments occurring at the Second Coming of Christ (a judgment of nations, a judgment of Jewish Tribulation survivors, a judgment of Gentile Tribulation survivors, a judgment of martyred Tribulation saints and so on), I think it makes more sense to see one judgment when Christ returns to earth:

> But when the Son of Man comes in His glory, and all the angels with Him, then He will sit on His glorious throne. All the nations will be gathered before Him; and He will separate them from one another, as the shepherd separates the sheep from the goats; and He will put the sheep on His right, and the goats on the left. Then the King will say to those on his right, "Come, you who are blessed of My Father, inherit the kingdom prepared for you from the foundation of the world. For I was hungry, and you gave me something to eat; I was thirsty, and you gave Me something to drink; I was a stranger, and you invited Me in. . . Truly I say to you, to the extent that you did it to one of these brothers of Mine, even the least of them, you did it to Me." Then He will also say to those on His left, "Depart from Me, accursed ones, into the eternal fire which has been prepared for the devil and his angels." (Matthew 25:31–35, 40–41)

As we saw in chapter 1, these verses are some of the most misunderstood and misapplied passages of Scripture. Contrary to popular opinion, this is not a general command to clothe, feed, and care for the neglected. Instead, it is an explanation of a specific judgment for a specific group of people (Tribulation survivors) that will occur when Christ returns to earth. Those who have given aid to the 144,000 Jewish witnesses (see chapter 5) will have demonstrated their faith in the gospel message and will be ushered into Christ's kingdom. Those who reject the ministry of the 144,000 will be cast into the lake of fire—the same lake of fire that will serve as the eternal destination of other unbelievers.

But what about the rest of us who are not a part of this judgment or the Great White Throne Judgment?

- Should we be concerned about God's evaluation of our lives?
- Is there a time when we will have to account for our words, actions, thoughts, and motivations even though we have experienced God's forgiveness of our sins?
- Does how we live our life now make any difference in the kind of eternity we will experience?

The answer to all of the above questions is "yes." One day every Christian will stand before Christ at an event referred to in Scripture as "the judgment seat of Christ."

The Reality of the Judgment Seat of Christ

Last year we took a group of church members to visit the ancient city of Corinth, where the apostle Paul ministered for eighteen months. Acts 18 tells us that many "were believing and being baptized" in Corinth because of Paul's ministry (v. 8). But many were also agitated by Paul's preaching, so they hauled him before the Roman proconsul Gallio to give an account for his actions:

"But while Gallio was proconsul of Achaia, the Jews with one accord rose up against Paul and brought him before the judgment seat" (Acts 18:12).

The word translated "judgment seat" is the Greek word *bema*. It refers to a raised platform on which a ruler or judge would sit to pronounce his decree. We actually stood on the spot where the apostle Paul faced Gallio as the Roman ruler who sat on the judgment seat. I imagined what it must have been like to stand, shackled in chains, before an indifferent ruler who, with a single word, could extinguish my life. But Paul never wavered in his determination to obey God and preach the gospel. What was the source of his unyielding courage? It was the realization that one day he would stand before another judgment seat and give an account of his life to the true Judge of the universe, the Lord Jesus Christ. Paul later used this imagery of the judgment seat in reminding the Corinthians of a coming evaluation of each of our lives:

Therefore we also have as our ambition, whether at home or absent, to be pleasing to Him. For we must all appear before the judgment seat of Christ, so that each one may be recompensed for his deeds in the body, according to what he has done, whether good or bad. (2 Corinthians 5:9–10)

Notice that Paul wrote "*We* must all appear," not "*They* must all appear." Paul is obviously including himself in this future judgment that will be reserved for Christians. Every believer will one day answer to Christ for every thought, word, action, and motivation of his earthly life. But unlike the Great White Throne Judgment, the purpose of this judgment is not condemnation, but evaluation and commendation.

A few years ago I went to the doctor for an extensive physical exam. For several hours I was poked, pinched, and prodded in just about every part of my anatomy. But for me the worst part of the test was being submerged in what was affectionately known as "the fat tank." The doctor had me remove all of my clothing and climb into a basket suspended above a pool of water. Then I was lowered into the water, holding my breath for a seemingly interminable amount of time while the doctor determined my percentage of body fat. If that wasn't bad enough, I was then forced to stand completely naked in front of the doctor while he used some kind of torture device to grab different parts of my body and calculate my body fat by a different method. Every chocolate chip cookie I had ever eaten, every morning I had rolled over in bed and said, "No exercise today," every late night trip to the refrigerator was suddenly on display to my physician.

At the end of the ordeal, the doctor had a conference with me in his office. After a few pleasantries, he opened the book containing the results of my exam. First, he commended me for the good things I had done: my exercise program, the results of the treadmill tests, and the bowl of Bran Flakes I consumed every morning. But then his smile turned to a frown. "Now, let's talk about your body fat. We need to shave a few percentage points off that. And your cholesterol needs to be lowered. You need to cut back on all of that coffee." The doctor commended me for the good things I had done and pointed out those things I could have done better without condemning me. His evaluation was based on a genuine care about my welfare.

Similarly, at the Judgment Seat of Christ (which probably occurs immediately after the Rapture) every aspect of our lives will be evaluated by Christ. Yet, many Christians have difficulty accepting that truth.

- "Doesn't becoming a Christian mean that all of my sins have been forgiven?"
- "I thought that when God forgave my mistakes He forgot them?"
- "Aren't my good works worthless before God?"

We will answer all of those questions in a moment. But first, let's establish the fact that Christians are indeed going to have their works—all of them—judged by Christ. First Corinthians 3:10–15 is the most detailed passage in the New Testament concerning the Judgment Seat of Christ. Notice what Paul says about the completeness of this judgment: "*each* man's work will become evident; for the day will show it because it is to be revealed with fire, and the fire itself will test the quality of each man's work" (1 Corinthians 3:13; emphasis mine).

Consider again Paul's words in 2 Corinthians 5:10:

"For we must all appear before the judgment seat of Christ, so that each one may be recompensed for his deeds in the body, according to what he has done, *whether good or bad*" (emphasis mine).

Both of these passages describe the completeness of this judgment. The *bema* judgment is for *every* Christian and will cover *all* of our works. There are continuing privacy concerns about search engines such as Google and Yahoo that have the ability to record the history of peoples' activities on the web. Just imagine a record somewhere of all of your Internet activity including every website you have ever visited, every article you have every read, or every communication you have ever sent.

God has a record of our every word, thought, action, and motivation, and one day He will bring them all to light. Some Christians reject this truth because they have been taught that neither their sins nor their good deeds make any difference to God once we become a Christian.

The Judgment Seat of Christ in no way invalidates the forgiveness we have received from Christ. As we saw in the last chapter, when we trust in Jesus Christ as our Savior, we are wrapping ourselves in the righteousness of Christ. (Remember the illustrations of the two books?) God no longer sees our sin, but He sees the perfection of His own Son. Nevertheless, the fact that we have been declared "not guilty" before God and are guaranteed a place in heaven does not negate the possibility of God's evaluation of our works. For example, consider King David's tryst with Bathsheba in the Old Testament and Ananias and Sapphira in the New Testament (the couple in the early church who were struck dead for lying, as recorded in Acts 5).

They were all believers who had been forgiven of their sins and are in heaven today. Yet their sins still carried serious consequences. Their salvation did not exempt them from God's evaluation of their lives.

For those who want to discount the importance of our works, we need to draw an important distinction. Though our works are worthless to secure our *place* in heaven, they will play a large role in determining our *rank* in heaven. The apostle Paul draws a distinction between works *before* salvation and works *after* salvation:

> For by grace you have been saved through faith; and that not of yourselves, it is the gift of God; not as a result of works, so that no one may boast. For we are His work-manship, created in Christ Jesus for good works, which God prepared beforehand so that we would walk in them. (Ephesians 2:8–10)

Before we become a Christian, our works are only sufficient to condemn us. But once we become a Christian, our works are of great importance to God. In the last section of this chapter we will discuss the specific relationship between our works in this present life and our future rewards throughout eternity.

THE BASIS FOR THE JUDGMENT SEAT OF CHRIST

By what standard will our works be evaluated at the Judgment Seat of Christ? Paul answers that question clearly in 1 Corinthians 3:

For no man can lay a foundation other than the one which is laid, which is Jesus Christ. Now if any man builds on the foundation with gold, silver, precious stones, wood, hay, straw, each man's work will become evident; for the day will show it because it is to be revealed with fire, and the fire itself will test the quality of each man's work. (1 Corinthians 3:11–13)

Imagine that your father, a multibillionaire, purchases two one-acre tracts of land for you and a sibling. He pours a foundation on each piece of land and then gives each of you one million dollars, with these instructions: "I am going to give you one year to build the most beautiful home you can construct. At the end of the year, the one who builds the most elaborate house will receive twice as much of my estate as the other." You and your sibling are thrilled with the possibility.

You begin work immediately. You hire architects to draw up the plans, you ask contractors for estimates, and you establish a rigid schedule to make sure you complete your work on time. When the deadline arrives, you have a home that rivals the Taj Mahal.

However, your sibling is not as industrious. Family responsibilities, work, and hobbies keep him from the task at hand. Not only that, but he has some immediate needs for that one million dollars: college tuition, a new car, and a swimming pool. The night before the deadline, he decides to get busy and construct the best home he can with little money and only a few hours of time. A grass hut is all he can manage to build.

The next morning, your father surveys the two homes. He praises you for your efforts and rewards you with the promise of a large portion of his vast estate. As he walks around your sibling's grass hut, however, he expresses his disappointment. As a result of procrastination and squandering of resources, your sibling forfeits billions of dollars of future wealth. He is still in the family, but he does not receive the same reward.

Paul says that when we become a Christian, we all have the same foundation for our lives: Jesus Christ. Nevertheless, we choose what kind of life we want to construct upon that foundation. Some choose to build palaces that will receive our heavenly Father's commendation. Others squander their time and resources and build grass huts that receive our Father's condemnation.

The apostle Paul explains two specific criteria by which our lives will be judged.

1. Our lives are judged on the basis of durability.

We can build our lives with "gold, silver, precious stones" or with "wood, hay, and straw." Obviously the former represents those things which are valuable and lasting. The latter category represents those things which are cheap and temporal.

Let's get specific. A life that is built around the pursuit of a career, or financial gain, or sensual delights is a life built with wood, hay, and straw. Such a life will not survive the fire of God's judgment. However, a life that is built around serving Christ, modeling His character, and building His kingdom is one that will stand the test of time.

What is the focus of your life? Having trouble answering that question? Then I invite you to honestly consider these questions:

- What do I think about most often?
- What do I talk about most often?
- If someone were to give me $100,000, how would I spend it?

Your response to those questions will quickly reveal whether your life is focused on that which is temporal or eternal. Are you building a life with gold, silver, and precious stones or with wood, hay, and straw?

2. Our lives are judged on the basis of motives.

Sometimes *why* we do something can be just as important as *what* we do. At the Judgment Seat of Christ, God will examine the "whys" as well as the "whats" of our lives:

> Therefore do not go on passing judgment before the time,
> but wait until the Lord comes who will both bring to light
> the things hidden in the darkness and disclose the *motives*
> of men's hearts; and then each man's praise will come to
> him from God. (1 Corinthians 4:5; emphasis mine)

If I share the gospel with a person out of a genuine concern for him, God counts that as "gold." However, if my motive is to exalt myself as a "soul-winner" to other Christians, that is labeled as "wood."

If I give my money to God as an act of worship and obedience, God views that as "silver." But if my motivation is recognition by others, my actions are deemed "straw." Proverbs 16:2 reminds us that "All the ways of a man are clean in his own sight, but the LORD weighs the motives."

One word of caution. Don't use this truth as a cop-out for dis-obedience. Some people rationalize their lack of faithfulness to Christ by saying, "If my heart is not in giving, witnessing, or service, then what is the point of doing it?" One of the purest motivations for obeying Christ is faith—faith that God is going to reward me for serving Him, even when my heart is not in it. Even though I really don't want to give my money to the church this month, I do so believing that God will one day reward my obedience. Although I may not feel like witnessing to my friend, I do so, believing that one day God will honor my efforts. Even though I would rather be at the lake on Sunday morning, I teach my first-grade Sunday school class believing that there will be future compensation for my service.

"Serving God for rewards is a wrong motivation," you say? Consider Abraham's motivation for obeying God and leaving his home in Ur: "for he was looking for the city which has founda-tions, whose architect and builder is God" (Hebrews 11:10). Or think about Moses, who chose "to endure ill-treatment with the people of God than to enjoy the passing pleasures of sin, consid-ering the reproach of Christ greater riches than the treasures of Egypt; for he was looking to the reward" (Hebrews 11: 25–26). The promise of a future reward was Abraham's and Moses' motivation for obedience.

The Results of the Judgment Seat of Christ

If I just make it into heaven, won't that be reward enough? Will the results of God's evaluation of our lives make any real difference in eternity? Paul doesn't hesitate in answering those questions. There are tangible and measurable consequences we will experience at the Judgment Seat of Christ:

> If any man's work which he has built on it remains, he will receive a reward. If any man's work is burned up, he will suffer loss; but he himself will be saved, yet so as through fire. (1 Corinthians 3:14–15)

1. Christians will receive rewards in heaven.

Those whose actions and motivations are deemed to be "silver, gold, and precious stones" will receive invaluable rewards. The Bible speaks of "crowns" which Christians will receive in heaven including the "crown of glory" (1 Peter 5:4) for those who serve in leadership in a church; the "crown of exultation" (1 Thessalonians 2:19–20) which is associated with evangelism; the "crown of life" (James 1:12, Revelation 2:10) which is reserved for those who endure the trials of life; and, "the crown of righteousness" which is bestowed on those who live obediently in anticipation of the Lord's return (2 Timothy 4:8). Some believe that these are actual crowns we will wear in heaven; however, others like myself see these crowns as symbolic of very real benefits given to those who succeed at the Judgment Seat of Christ. Those benefits include:

Privileges. When our girls were little we made several treks to Disney World. If you have ever been, you know that for a single price you can enter the park and enjoy all of the attractions. However, those who are willing to pay more can have some additional benefits: early entrance into the park, nicer accommodations, a chance to eat breakfast with Mickey and Minnie.

In the same way, the Bible teaches that some Christians will enjoy special benefits in heaven including a special entrance into the kingdom of God (2 Peter 1:11), special access to the tree of life (Revelation 2:7); and even special treatment by Christ Himself (Luke 12:37).[2] I don't pretend to understand what all of these benefits mean, but they are nevertheless real and worth attaining.

Praise. Can you recall a time when your parent said to you, "I'm so proud of you. You are a wonderful daughter (or son)"? Has your employer ever pulled you aside and said, "You're doing a great job. I appreciate all you do for this organization"? Such affirmations can keep you going for weeks! Now, imagine hearing the Creator of the Universe say to you, "Well done, good and faithful servant!" That is a reward that will be reserved for obedient Christians (Matthew 25:21 NIV).

Positions. If you think praise is cheap, then consider the benefits that will accompany those words of praise from the Master: "Well done, good and faithful slave. You were faithful with a few things, I will put you in charge of many things; enter into the joy of your master" (Matthew 25:21).

Jesus is teaching that our faithfulness in this life will determine what responsibility we have in the new heaven and earth. Paul declared the same truth in 2 Timothy 2:12: "If we endure, we will also reign with Him." One day we will be corulers with Christ over the angels, the planets, and the nations.

Most of us fail to grasp the vastness of God's creation. The Milky Way galaxy in which our solar system resides contains 200 to 400 billion stars. But our galaxy is only one of 100 to 200 billion galaxies in the universe. The Hubble telescope has relayed from space images of galaxies that are 12 billion times 6 trillion miles away![3] God will delegate to us varying degrees of responsibility for governing this immense universe for all eternity based on our faithfulness in serving Christ during our brief seventy years of life on Earth.

I know what you are saying: "I'm tired. The last thing I want in heaven is *more* responsibility. I just want to float on a cloud somewhere and take it easy. That will be enough for me." Think again. The book of Genesis tells us that we were designed in God's image to work and rule, just as Adam and Eve did. God meant for us to be invigorated, not debilitated, by labor. Only after sin entered the world did work become tedious and difficult. But in the new creation, all the hindrances to enjoying work will be removed: tired bodies, inadequate compensation, and soured relationships. We will enjoy the responsibility God gives us, but the degree of fulfillment we experience will depend upon our faithfulness to Christ in this life.

Whatever these crowns represent, the Word of God teaches that they represent rewards that are definitely worth pursuing.

2. Some Christians will experience loss of rewards.

Unfortunately, the Judgment Seat of Christ will also result in a loss of rewards for other Christians:

"If any man's work is burned up, he will suffer loss; but he himself will be saved, yet so as through fire" (1 Corinthians 3:15).

Don't allow anyone to mislead you. Not every Christian will experience the same degree of joy and satisfaction in eternity. Those who have built their lives around trivial pursuits will experience real, measurable loss in the next life. Although their salvation is secure ("he himself will be saved"), they will endure real and lasting regret as they see what could have been theirs had they invested their lives in building God's kingdom rather than their own.

When I have taught on this subject before, some people have objected, saying, "What you are describing sounds like hell instead of heaven. If heaven is a place of joy, how is it that some Christians will also experience regret over the loss of rewards?"

Perhaps this analogy will help you understand how the next life will be a mixture of both joy and regret for some Christians. One year my insurance agent said, "Robert, I've been reviewing your homeowner's policy, and I believe you are underinsured by fifty thousand dollars. I would recommend that you increase your coverage."

But what if I had said, "Let me think about it and I'll get back to you in a few weeks"?

That very night Amy and I are awakened by the smell of smoke. Hearing the screams of our two girls, we stumble through the thick fog until we reach their bedrooms. Grabbing our daughters, we grope through the darkness searching for a way out. But all of the exits are blocked, so we throw a chair through the window and climb through the broken glass. Once safely outside, we watch in horror as our home is consumed by the flames.

What emotions would I feel at that moment? Certainly I would be relieved that my family made it through the fire. No one could place a price tag on their lives. Nevertheless, I would also feel a deep sense of regret as I considered the financial loss I was about to experience because I made a wrong choice about my insurance. My joy of survival would be tempered by my feelings of regret.[4]

The apostle Paul is saying that at the judgment of Christ all Christians will feel overwhelming gratitude for escaping the flames of hell. But that gratitude will be tempered with a sense of loss as some believers realize what rewards might have been theirs had they lived more faithfully for God.

One popular writer relates the story of a beggar in India who saw a wealthy raja come toward him, riding in his beautiful chariot. The beggar stood by the side of the road, holding out his bowl of rice, hoping for a handout. To his surprise, the rajah stopped and demanded, "Give me some of your rice!" The beggar was angry at the thought of such a wealthy man demanding some of his scarce supply of rice. He begrudgingly gave the rajah one grain of rice. "I want more." So the beggar gave him another grain. "More rice, please," the rajah asked. By now, the beggar was seething with resentment, but he handed him one more grain of rice.

After the rajah departed, the beggar looked into the bowl of rice and noticed something glittering. It was a grain of gold, the size of a grain of rice. He looked more carefully and found two more grains of gold. For every grain of rice he had given, he had received a grain of gold in return.

The writer then draws this application: "If we clutch our bowl of rice, we shall lose our reward. If we are faithful and give God each grain, He gives us gold in return. And the gold God gives will survive the fire."[5]

It is the promise of that future reward that motivated the apostle Paul to write,

Therefore we also have as our ambition, whether at home or absent, to be pleasing to Him. For we must all appear before the judgment seat of Christ, so that each one may be recompensed for his deeds in the body, according to what he has done, whether good or bad. (2 Corinthians 5:9–10)

Chapter Ten

||||||||||||||||||||||||||||||||||||

THE TRUTH
ABOUT ETERNITY

I love the story Harold Kushner tells about a man who died after living a godless, immoral life. To his surprise, however, the newly departed found himself in a world of bright sunlight, soft music, and people all dressed in white.

"I sure never expected to end up here," he mused to himself. "I suppose God must have a soft spot in His heart for people like me."

He turned to one of the figures in white and said, "Can I buy you a drink? I've got something to celebrate."

The figure replied, "If you are referring to an alcoholic beverage, we don't serve that here."

"No booze, huh? Well, how about a game of poker? Poker, Black Jack, you name it, we'll play."

"Sorry," the figure dressed in white said, "We don't gamble here either."

The man was mystified. "Then what do you do all day around here?"

"Well, we read the Psalms a lot. There is a Bible study every morning and a prayer meeting every afternoon."

"Psalms? Bible study? Prayer meetings? Heaven isn't what it's cracked up to be."

At this point the figure in white smiled and said, "I see that you don't understand. We're in heaven; you're in hell."[1]

Cute story, but very misleading. The popular consensus is that all people, regardless of their spiritual convictions, will end up in the same location after they die.

Even popular Christian writers such as Rob Bell suggest that heaven and hell are more a matter of perception than location. Bell (mis)uses the parable of the prodigal son to support his claim, noting that at the end of the story the younger son was happy and the older son was miserable, but both were in their father's house. Bell then extrapolates from this story the erroneous belief that heaven and hell are in actuality the same place:

"In this story, heaven and hell are within each other, intertwined, interwoven, bumping up against each other."[2]

Contrary to the claims of Bell and others, the Bible teaches that there are two very different destinies awaiting individuals after they die. Jesus affirmed this truth when He said,

> Enter through the narrow gate; for the gate is wide and the
> way is broad that leads to destruction, and there are many
> who enter through it. For the gate is small and the way
> is narrow that leads to life, and there are few who find it.
> (Matthew 7:13–14)

Two gates, two roads, two destines. Up to this point, we have tracked the future of both believers and unbelievers in God's prophetic plan. We have seen that when a Christian dies, his spirit goes immediately to be with Christ, and his body will be resurrected at a specific time according to God's order: some at the Rapture, others at the Second Coming, and the remainder at the end of the Millennium. Not only will these Christians be resurrected, but they will also be rewarded—again, at different times. Believers living in this present age (often referred to as the Church Age) will be evaluated at the Judgment Seat of Christ, which apparently takes place immediately after the Rapture. Other believers will be rewarded at times not specified in Scripture. But all believers will share the same future: resurrected bodies, eternal rewards, and a recreated heaven and earth.

Sadly, unbelievers will not share in that future. Although some unbelievers (those who survive the Tribulation) will be judged at the Second Coming of Christ and cast into the eternal lake of fire, the majority of unbelievers will be raised from the dead prior to the Great White Throne Judgment described in Revelation 20:11–15. Because of their unwillingness to trust in Christ as their Savior, they will be judged by their works and cast into the eternal lake of fire where they "will be tormented day and night forever and ever" just like the beast, false prophet, and Satan who are already there (Revelation 20:10).

In this chapter we are going to examine more closely what is often referred to as "the eternal state." What is hell going to be like for unbelievers? What can believers anticipate in heaven?

THE TRUTH ABOUT HELL

I find it fascinating that many people who readily accept the idea of heaven just as easily dismiss the biblical teaching about hell. Robert Ingersoll, the famous lawyer and atheist in the nineteenth century, once delivered a scorching (pardon the pun) lecture on the absurdity of hell. He labeled hell as "the scarecrow of religion" and told his audience how unscientific the whole concept was. Most intelligent people, Ingersoll claimed, had long ago abandoned belief in hell. A drunk approached Ingersoll after the talk and said, "Bob, I liked your lecture about hell. But I want you to be sure about it, because I'm depending on you."[3]

Unfortunately many people are banking their eternal destiny on the wrong people. Instead of listening to the "logic" of people like Ingersoll, we should consider the words of the only Person who is capable of describing what *really* awaits us beyond the grave.

Jesus Christ had a great deal to say about the reality of hell. In fact, He spoke more often about hell than He did about heaven. The Lord's most extensive discourse about hell is found in Luke 16:

> Now there was a rich man, and he habitually dressed in purple and fine linen, joyously living in splendor every day. And a poor man named Lazarus was laid at his gate, covered with sores, and longing to be fed with the crumbs which were falling from the rich man's table; besides,

even the dogs were coming and licking his sores. Now the poor man died and was carried away by the angels to Abraham's bosom; and the rich man also died and was buried. In Hades he lifted up his eyes, being in torment, and saw Abraham far away and Lazarus in his bosom. And he cried out and said, "Father Abraham, have mercy on me, and send Lazarus so that he may dip the tip of his finger in water and cool off my tongue, for I am in agony in this flame." But Abraham said, "Child, remember that during your life you received your good things, and likewise Lazarus bad things; but now he is being comforted here, and you are in agony. And besides all this, between us and you there is a great chasm fixed, so that those who wish to come over from here to you will not be able, and that none may cross over from there to us." (Luke 16:19–26)

The New Testament uses three words to describe the destination of non-Christians. While all three of these words are translated as "hell" in many English versions of the Bible, the three Greek words denote very different places. First, the word *Tartaros* (used only in 2 Peter 2:4) describes the place of judgment of the wicked angels described in Jude 6. The second word, *Gehenna*, is used twelve times in the New Testament and primarily refers to the eternal lake of fire (Revelation 19:20; 20:10; 20:15) that will be the final residence of all unbelievers. The third word for *hell* is the one found in the Luke 16 passage:

Hades. The term *Hades* is used to describe the temporary location of the unsaved dead who are awaiting the Great White Throne Judgment. You will remember that at this judgment the residents of Hades are resurrected and eventually dispatched to the lake of fire (*Gehenna*).[4]

Although Jesus is specifically describing Hades in this parable (which may have been an actual incident), we can assume that the horrors of Hades are also characteristic of the eternal lake of fire. Thus, from this point on we will use the general term *hell* to describe both the immediate and the eternal residence of unbelievers. What did Jesus teach about hell?

1. Hell is a place of physical torment.

The rich man begged Abraham for mercy because he was "in agony in this flame" (Luke 16:24). There is a growing belief in a doctrine called annihilationism, which theorizes that unbelievers are judged and then destroyed, instead of being tormented for eternity. While such a belief may be comforting, it is not accurate. Jesus is warning that unbelievers will face an eternity of indescribable suffering. Most of us have experienced excruciating pain before, but eventually relief came. But in hell there will be no relief. The awful truth of hell is that when a person has spent ten billion years there, he will not have reduced by one second the amount of time he has left in that horrible place. That is why hell will be a place of unending weeping, wailing, and gnashing of teeth (Luke 13:28).

2. Hell is a place of indescribable loneliness.

The Bible teaches that hell is place of darkness (Matthew 8:12). Have you ever heard people say, "I want to go to hell so I can party with my friends"? Forget it. There will be no socializing in hell because no one will be able to see anyone or anything. Writer John Thomas has vividly described the horror of hell through the eyes of an unbeliever who has just found himself in this awful place:

> After a roar of physical pain blasts him, he spends his first moments wailing and gnashing his teeth. But after a season, he grows accustomed to the pain, not that it's become tolerable, but that his capacity for it has enlarged to comprehend it, yet not be consumed by it. Though he hurts, he is now able to think, and he instinctively looks about him. But as he looks, he sees only blackness. . . .
>
> He hangs there, alone with his pain. Unable to touch a solid object or see a solitary thing, he begins to weep. His sobs choke through the darkness. They become weak. Then lost in hell's roar.[5]

3. Hell is a place of no return.

Some writers like Rob Bell want to suggest that hell—whatever it may be—is only temporary. According to this theory, hell will be a "period of pruning" and "an intense experience of correction" for those who have rejected God's love in this life.[6] However, God will use the experience of hell to win over unbelievers so that they can eventually accept God's love and experience the same heaven as Christians forever:

"No one can resist God's pursuit forever because God's love will eventually melt even the hardest hearts."[7]

While the thought of a second chance after death for unbelievers to repent is comforting, it is also contradictory to Jesus' teaching that hell is a forever destination. Perhaps the most disturbing aspect of hell is that once there, no occupant is able to leave for any reason. In Jesus' story, the rich man begged Abraham to cross over into Hades and relieve him of his torment or at least send someone to warn the rich man's siblings of the horrors of Hades. But Abraham reminded him that "between us and you there is a great chasm fixed, so that those who wish to come over from here to you will not be able, and that none may cross over from there to us" (Luke 16:26). Once we die our eternal destination is just that—*eternal*.

While most people today use digital cameras and smartphones to take pictures, a few die-hard photography enthusiasts still use film. Once film is exposed it is placed in a developing solution. As long as a negative remains in the developing solution it can be altered somewhat. But there comes a time in the developing process when you drop the film in a solution called the "stop bath." As soon as the film hits the stop bath, the image on the film is permanently fixed.

Death is the "stop bath" for every person. Before we die, we have an infinite number of opportunities to alter the course of our life and eternity. But the moment we die, all opportunity to change is over.

As the writer of Hebrews notes, "it is appointed for men to die once and after this comes judgment" (Hebrews 9: 27). No second chances after death, only judgment. Isn't it unfair for God not to offer the occupants of hell a chance to repent after they die? As one writer notes, "Fairness doesn't demand God give people a second chance after death, since he gives us thousands of chances before death."[8]

Hell is an eternal destination. The Bible uses the same word—*forever*—to describe the eternality both of heaven and hell (see Revelation 22:5 and Revelation 20:10). That means that if you diminish by one second the amount of time unbelievers spend in hell then you must equally reduce the amount of time Christians spend in heaven. Again, John Thomas captures the horror of the eternality of hell for the new occupant of hell:

> So he casts about in his mind for a plan. . . . *Of course*, he thinks, *Jesus, the God of love, can get me out of this.*
>
> He cries out with a surge, "Jesus! Jesus! You were right! Help me! Get me out of this!"
>
> He waits, breathing hard with desperation. The sound of his voice slips into the darkness and is lost.
>
> He tries again, "I believe, Jesus! I believe now! Save me from this!" Again the darkness smothers his words.
>
> Our sinner is not unique. Everyone in hell believes.[9]

I think it would be appropriate to move from the academic to the practical. Are you absolutely certain that if you were to die that you would escape the horrors of hell that Jesus so vividly described?

Can you point to a time in your life when you placed your faith in the Lord Jesus Christ to save you from your sins?

What about the spiritual condition of your friends or family members? When you think of those people who sit across the breakfast table from you every morning, can you say with certainty that they will escape hell? I often think of the words of Martin Marty, renowned professor at the University of Chicago, about the reality of hell: "If people really believed in hell, they wouldn't be watching basketball games or even the television preachers. They would be out rescuing people."[10]

THE OTHER SIDE OF THE STORY

Fortunately, God has provided a way of escape from hell, and those who choose to enter through it will experience an eternity beyond what our finite minds can fathom. I have often wondered why the Bible does not give us more specific information about heaven. Perhaps it is because of our limited ability to comprehend such information. Or possibly God understands that such information would only increase our level of discontent with our earthly life.

Imagine that you call your child to dinner. On the plate in front of him are spinach, meat, and carrots—all the things he should eat. But sitting right beside his plate is a beautiful strawberry shortcake, covered with whipped cream. It would be difficult for any child (and many adults!) to eat spinach with a strawberry shortcake in full view. If we had a clear picture of all the splendors of heaven that awaited us, we might find it difficult to concentrate on our responsibilities in this life.[11] Nevertheless, God gives us just enough information about heaven to whet our appetites for the future.

THE TOP TEN QUESTIONS ABOUT HEAVEN

What does the Bible reveal about heaven? Once a year our church devotes a Sunday evening service to a program we call "Ask the Pastor." Church members are given the opportunity to pose any question they choose to yours truly. It is always a fun experience and is our most attended evening service of the year (people love to see their pastor squirm). Since many of the questions I am asked have to do with heaven, I thought you might be interested in the answers to the ten most frequently asked questions about the eternal state for believers.

1. Is heaven an actual place or simply a state of mind?

The Bible goes to great lengths to demonstrate that heaven is a definite place. In John 14 Jesus twice refers to heaven as a "place" (the Greek word is *topos* denoting a specific location).

> In My Father's house are many dwelling places; if it were not so, I would have told you; for I go to prepare a *place* for you. If I go and prepare a *place* for you, I will come again and receive you to Myself, that where I am, there you may be also. (John 14:2–3; emphasis mine)

In the above passage Jesus also describes heaven as being filled with "dwelling places," which again indicates that heaven is a definite location. Also, consider the description of Jesus' ascension into heaven:

> And after He had said these things, He was lifted up while they were looking on, and a cloud received Him out of their sight. And as they were gazing intently into the sky while He was going, behold, two men in white clothing stood beside them. They also said, "Men of Galilee, why do you stand looking into the sky? This Jesus, who has been taken up from you into heaven, will come in just the same way as you have watched Him go into heaven." (Acts 1:9–11)

When Jesus ascended into "heaven" where did He go? Did he ascend from reality to a "state of mind"? Of course not. The Bible is teaching that heaven is a real location.[12]

2. Where do Christians go when they die?

The Bible clearly teaches that when a Christian dies, he is "at home with the Lord" (2 Corinthians 5:8). While we often use the term "heaven" to refer to the destination of believers who die, it is not entirely accurate to do so. Our final heavenly home (the one referred to by Jesus in John 14 and described by John in Revelation 21–22) is still "under construction." Just as most unbelievers will not be cast into the lake of fire until after the Great White Throne

Judgment, believers will not see the new heaven and earth God is constructing until after the destruction of the present heaven and earth described by the apostle Peter:

> But the day of the Lord will come like a thief, in which the heavens will pass away with a roar and the elements will be destroyed with intense heat, and the earth and its works will be burned up. (2 Peter 3:10)

The apostle John saw the new heaven and the new earth only after "the first heaven and the first earth passed away" (Revelation 21:1).

3. Are you implying then that when people die they go to a kind of purgatory until the end of time?

Not at all. As we saw in the parable of the rich man and Lazarus, when people die they go to a place known as "Hades." Until the resurrection of Christ, Hades was divided into two compartments: the place of torment for unbelievers (the destination of the rich man) and "Abraham's bosom" (the destination of Lazarus). When an unbeliever dies, he immediately experiences unbearable torment as he awaits his final judgment at the Great White Throne. After that judgment he is cast into the eternal lake of fire.

When a Christian dies, he immediately experiences the joy of being in God's presence until the time that he inhabits the new heaven and the new earth.

There are some Bible scholars who believe that Hades is still divided into "Abraham's bosom" for Christians and the "place of torment" for unbelievers. Others believe that after the resurrection of Christ, the Lord emptied the compartment known as "Abraham's bosom" and brought its inhabitants into His presence. Thus, today the term "Hades" refers only to the temporary—but nevertheless horrific—dwelling place of unbelievers. When Christians die, they go into the presence of God, wherever that might be.

What we do know with certainty is this: When unbelievers die they immediately begin to suffer; when Christians die, they are immediately transported into God's presence.

4. What is the difference between the Millennial Kingdom and the new heaven and new earth described in Revelation 21–22?

The Millennial Kingdom will involve a renovation of the present earth. But after the Great White Throne Judgment, the present heaven and earth will be completely destroyed (2 Peter 3:7), and God will unveil His new heaven and earth. Look at John's description of this new heaven and earth:

> Then I saw a new heaven and a new earth; for the first heaven and the first earth passed away, and there is no longer any sea. And I saw the holy city, new Jerusalem, coming down out of heaven from God, made ready as a bride adorned for her husband. (Revelation 21:1–2)

The final destination for Christians will be this "new Jerusalem" that John saw descending from heaven to the new earth. When John first views this magnificent city, it is already complete. I like to refer to the new Jerusalem as the ultimate in pre-fab housing! The Bible teaches that currently this city is being constructed under the supervision of Jesus Christ ("I go to prepare a place for you" Jesus promised in John 14:2), and at God's appointed time this city will descend to the new earth.

Revelation 21–22 gives us many details about this city: its great wall, its twelve gates, the twelve foundation stones, the absence of night or the sea, and the tree of life that shall provide healing for the nations. But one of the most interesting aspects of the city is its size. John describes the city as a cube that is fifteen hundred miles long, wide, and high (Revelation 21:16). If these measurements are to be understood literally (and the specificity of the measurements argues for a literal interpretation), then we are talking about a very large city!

My predecessor, Dr. W. A. Criswell, noted that such a city would stretch from Maine to Florida and would cover all of Ireland, Great Britain, France, Spain, Germany, Austria, Italy, Turkey, and half of Russia.[13] Additionally, there is no reason to think that Christians will be confined to this earthly city, given the supernatural bodies we will possess. We will be free to roam the universe. So you can quit worrying that there will not be enough room in heaven for you and everyone you want to bring with you!

5. What kind of bodies will we have in heaven? Will we know one another in heaven?

Our heavenly bodies will be both superior and, at the same time, similar to our present bodies. In 1 Corinthians 15, Paul uses an agricultural analogy to illustrate this truth. When a farmer plants a seed into the ground, the seed actually dies. Miraculously, that decomposed seed produces a harvest that is superior to, and yet also similar to, the original seed.

Have you ever thought how amazing it is that a tiny seed planted into the ground can eventually become a large watermelon? The harvest is certainly superior to the seed (on a hot summer day would you rather eat a cold watermelon or a watermelon seed?), and yet the harvest is similar to the seed. You don't plant a watermelon seed and harvest a kumquat.

Similarly, our present bodies must die before we can reap the harvest of our new bodies. Although our new bodies will be superior to our present ones (just as a watermelon is to a watermelon seed), there will nevertheless be some similarities between the two.

Jesus' resurrection body illustrates the continuity that will exist between our new bodies and our old ones. Jesus' new body was certainly superior to His old one. Read Luke 24 and you will discover that Jesus' resurrection body was not limited by time and space. He could travel through walls and doors. And yet, He was not just a spirit, but possessed flesh and bones that the disciples could actually touch. Amazingly, Jesus enjoyed eating in His new body (which gives me hope that just possibly there will be Häagen-Dazs ice cream in heaven).

Jesus' new body apparently retained some of the physical characteristics of His earthly body, since His disciples recognized Him. That is why we can safely assume that we, too, will recognize one another in heaven. Our bodies will not be identical to one another, but will retain some of the unique characteristics of our previous bodies.

Many years ago I visited the Boeing aircraft company in Seattle, Washington, and saw the huge assembly line where those gigantic aircraft are manufactured. Before the assembly line ever starts producing airplanes, however, the designers must build the first plane, called a "prototype." After the prototype has been built, the other planes are patterned after the first one. The apostle Paul describes Jesus Christ as the "firstborn from the dead" (Colossians 1:18). The Greek word translated "firstborn" is the same word from which we derive our English word *prototype*. The Bible tells us that Jesus' resurrection body was a prototype of the bodies we will one day receive: bodies that are superior, and yet similar, to our present ones.

6. What age will we be in heaven?

Although I always anticipate this question at our annual "Ask the Pastor" session, this year I was surprised by a unique variation of it. A young woman stood at the microphone and asked, "If a woman is pregnant at the Rapture, will she be pregnant throughout eternity?" I paused and joked, "Yes—it's called hell!" After the laughter subsided, I had to admit that I don't know the answer to that question. Will embryos on earth be embryos in heaven? Will children on earth remain children in the new world? Will the American Association for Retired People have a branch office inside the pearly gates?

Obviously the real question is, "What age will we be in heaven?" Some have theorized that we will be the same age as the Lord when He began His earthly ministry—thirty years old. But the truth is that the Bible is silent on this topic.

7. Will there be animals in heaven?

At the Second Coming, Jesus Christ is described as returning to earth on a "white horse" (Revelation 19:11). Those of us who return with Him are described as "following Him on white horses" (Revelation 19:14). During Christ's thousand-year reign on the earth (the Millennium) the Bible describes the presence of animals on the renovated earth: the wolf, lamb, calf, and lion (Isaiah 11:6–9).

However, there is no specific mention of animals in the new heaven and the new earth, once the present heaven and earth are destroyed. If God chooses to place animals on the new earth, they will not be our present pets in resurrected bodies.

Ancient civilizations believed in the resurrection of household pets and placed replicas of those pets in the tombs of the deceased. But there is no indication in Scripture that animals possess eternal spirits that can be redeemed. In fact, Solomon says that the primary difference between human beings and animals is that humans have a spirit that transcends death. While both animals and humans experience the same fate (death), only man has a spirit ("breath") that ascends "upward" (into God's presence) after death (see Ecclesiastes 3:19–21).

8: Will there be marriage in heaven?

Jesus clearly answered this question. A group of Sadducees (who did not even believe in the afterlife) played their own version of "Ask the Rabbi" by posing this question to Jesus: "If a woman has seven different husbands in this life, whose wife will she be in heaven?" Jesus replied,

> The sons of this age marry and are given in marriage, but those who are considered worthy to attain to that age and the resurrection from the dead, neither marry nor are given in marriage; for they cannot even die anymore, because they are like angels, and are sons of God, being sons of the resurrection. (Luke 20:34–36)

Please note that Jesus did not say we *become* angels when we die, but in heaven we will share one similarity with the angels: we will not marry. You may not think you could enjoy heaven without marriage. Others may be more upset at the prospect of not having Fido with them in heaven! But remember, heaven is going to be a place of incomparable joy for every believer, meaning that God will provide everything we need for our happiness.

9. What will we do in heaven?

The image of Christians floating on clouds and plucking a harp throughout eternity is popular, but inaccurate. Even among Christians there is the mistaken belief that heaven will be one continuous worship service in which we bow down before God day and night forever and ever. Recently a guest preacher in our church said, "If you have trouble sitting through a two-hour worship service here on earth, you will be miserable in heaven because all we are going to do for eternity is praise God." There were some scattered "Amens" in the audience, but the lack of a roaring affirmation from the crowd indicated that many thought this concept of heaven bordered on the boring—and with good reason.

Yes, worship will be a primary activity in the new heaven and earth, but it will not be our *only* activity. Think back to the Garden of Eden in which the first man and woman lived in perfect communion with God untainted by sin. Was their only activity in the garden singing hymns and praying? Adam and Eve enjoyed an intimate relationship with God, filled with gratitude for all He had given them, while at the same time performing the task He had assigned them of cultivating the garden He had created (Genesis 2:15). Worship and work were not mutually exclusive activities in Eden; neither will they be in the new heaven and the new earth.

Since God originally created the first couple to be workers in His creation, we can assume that we will be busy in God's new world performing whatever tasks God gives us. The parable of the talents found in Matthew 25 indicates that we will be assigned responsibilities for ruling over cities, planets, and galaxies according to our faithfulness to God in this life. Fortunately, the impediments to the enjoyment of our work in this life will be removed in the next life.

10. Are Christians in heaven aware of what is happening on the earth?

Many people cite Hebrews 12:1 as evidence that deceased believers are peering over heaven's balcony and watching our every action:

"Therefore, since we have so great a cloud of witnesses surrounding us, let us also lay aside every encumbrance and the sin which so easily entangles us . . ."

However, the context of this verse demonstrates that the "cloud of witnesses" is a reference to the heroes of the faith mentioned in Hebrews 11. The writer is saying, "In light of their example of faith, we should persevere in our faith."

Nevertheless, there are some indications that people in heaven have an understanding of what is taking place on earth. Abraham was aware of the rich man's suffering in Hades (Luke 16), and the Tribulation saints will be aware of God's temporary restraint of judgment against the evil being committed on the earth (Revelation 6:10). The apostle Paul indicated that our perspective in this life is limited, but one day we "will know fully" (1 Corinthians 13:12). I would assume that such perfect knowledge would include a full awareness of all that is happening on earth.

A related question is, "Will Christians experience grief in heaven?" If Christians in heaven possess a full knowledge of events on earth, as well as the eternal damnation of some of our loved ones at the Great White Throne Judgment, doesn't that mean that there will be tears in heaven?

Revelation 21:4 promises that "[God] will wipe away every tear from their eyes; and there will no longer be any death; there will no longer be any mourning, or crying, or pain; the first things have passed away." Remember that the setting for this verse is *after* the Judgment Seat of Christ, the Great White Throne Judgment, and the destruction of the present heaven and earth. God promises that whatever sorrow may have accrued through those events will ultimately be resolved.

Just think: no more failed relationships, no more all-night vigils at the hospital, no more standing over the open grave of a loved one, no more crying or pain. I don't know about you, but that thought makes me want to push aside the spinach and grab some of that strawberry shortcake!

Obviously, God is not ready for us to do that just yet. He has given us some responsibilities in this world that must be fulfilled before we can enjoy the next world. In fact, the unpleasantness of this life will serve to make heaven taste that much better. But the opposite is true as well. The assurance of a better world should improve the taste of this one.

One of the most frequent criticisms of studying Bible prophecy is that it has no relevance to everyday life. You have probably heard the cliché, "It is possible to be so heavenly-minded that you are of no earthly good." Yet, the Bible never divorces the hope of the next life from our responsibility in this one. The apostle Peter wrote,

"Since all these things are to be destroyed in this way, what sort of people ought you to be in holy conduct and godliness, looking for and hastening the coming of the day of God" (2 Peter 3:11–12).

Shouldn't the truth of the Rapture discourage us from worshipping money since one day we will be forced to leave it all behind? Shouldn't the reality of the Great White Throne Judgment motivate us to share the message of Christ with those around us? Shouldn't the certainty of the Judgment Seat of Christ impact how we invest our time and energy right now?

I close with these words of C.S. Lewis about the value of being "heavenly-minded":

> Hope is one of the theological virtues. This means that a continual looking forward to the eternal world is not (as some moderns think) a form of escapism or wishful thinking, but one of the things a Christian is meant to do. It does not mean that we are to leave the present world as it is. If you read history you will find that the Christians who did most for the present world were just those who thought most of the next. It is since Christians have largely ceased to think of the other world that they have become so ineffective in this one. Aim at heaven and you will get earth "thrown in'; aim at earth and you will get neither.[14]

Anticipation of the "perfect ending" that awaits us is the most powerful motivation I know of for living a God-centered life . . . beginning today.

STUDY QUESTIONS

Chapter One: Why Study Prophecy?

1. What are the most common reasons people avoid studying prophecy? Which of these excuses have you used?
2. How would you answer someone who said, "Studying prophecy is a waste of time since the Bible says no one can know when Christ will return"?
3. Does the fact that there are a variety of opinions about end-time events make the study of prophecy futile? Why or why not?
4. Briefly summarize the three reasons, found in this chapter, for studying prophecy.
5. Give one example in which an understanding of end-time events could impact your everyday life.
6. Give one example in which a clear understanding of prophecy would assist you in interpreting a passage of Scripture accurately.
7. Why did you purchase this book? What do you hope this study of prophecy will do for you?

Chapter Two: It Begins and Ends with Israel

1. According to the author, what is the major theme of the Bible (Genesis 12–Revelation 22)?

2. What does the story of Abraham teach us about God's grace?

3. What are the three ingredients of God's promise to Abraham? Briefly describe each one.

4. Explain what Abraham understood about a coming Savior. Support your answer with Scripture.

5. Explain the term *reckon* as it relates to Christ's death. How would you illustrate this concept to a nine-year-old?

6. List and briefly explain the three characteristics of God's covenant with Abraham.

7. Why should we care whether or not God keeps His promises to Israel?

8. Of all of God's promises, which one is the most important to you? Why?

Chapter Three: Getting the Big Picture

1. Arrange these end-time events in the correct order (according to the viewpoint presented in this chapter). Place 1 by the first event, 2 by the second event, and so on.

        ____*Second Coming of Christ*

        ____*Tribulation*

        ____*The Church Age*

        ____*Eternity*

        ____*The Millennium*

        ____*The Rapture*

        ____*The Great White Throne Judgment*

2. Have you ever studied Bible prophecy before? Why or why not?

3. Now that you have read this chapter, see if you can give a one-or two-sentence explanation for each of these terms:

   Church Age:
   Rapture:
   Tribulation:
   Second Coming:
   Millennium:
   Great White Throne Judgment:
   Eternity:

4. How did Jesus answer His disciples' questions about the end-times? What can we learn from His reply?

Chapter Four: Not Left Behind

1. Explain the "mystery" that the apostle Paul unveiled.

2. Why didn't the Old Testament writers of Jesus mention the Rapture?

3. How has Israel's rejection of Christ benefited those of us who are Gentiles?

4. Cite one significant difference between the Rapture and the Second Coming of Christ.

5. In your own words summarize what will take place at the Rapture.

6. Does cremation or organ donation jeopardize our new bodies in heaven? Why or why not?

7. Briefly explain the differing views of the Rapture. Which view do you believe? Why?

8. Four arguments are given for a Pretribulation Rapture of the Church. Which of these arguments seems most convincing to you?

Chapter Five: When All Hell Breaks Loose

1. What important information does Daniel 9 reveal about the Tribulation?

2. What occurs between the first 483 years and the final seven years of God's plan for Israel?

3. Define "the day of the Lord."

4. What do we learn about "the day of the Lord" from 1 Thessalonians 5:1–4?

5. The author described the Tribulation as occurring in three "acts." Summarize the action of each of these acts:

    Act One: The Beginning

    Act Two: The Middle

    Act Three: The Final Half of the Tribulation

6. What are God's two purposes for the Tribulation?

7. How is God's mercy demonstrated through the 144,000 Jewish witnesses?

8. In one or two sentences, summarize the activity of the Antichrist during the Tribulation.

Chapter Six: History's Most Important Event

1. Briefly summarize the events we have studied so far in this book, including:

> *The Abrahamic Covenant:*
> *The Church Age:*
> *The Rapture:*
> *The Tribulation:*

2. What will be the human explanation for the battle called Armageddon? What will be the divine purpose for this conflict?
3. Describe what Christians will do at Armageddon.
4. Why do some people view the Rapture and Second Coming of Christ as the same event?
5. Cite three or four the differences between the Rapture and Second Coming.
6. Why is a literal return of Jesus Christ to earth important?
7. What excites you most about the Second Coming of Christ? Why?

Chapter Seven: Heaven on Earth

1. Define the word *Millennium:*

2. What reasons does the author give for believing in a literal thousand-year reign of Christ?

3. Briefly summarize these three views:

   premillennialism:
   postmillennialism:
   amillennialism:

4. Which viewpoint best expresses your belief? Why?

5. What do you see as the major problem with your particular millennial viewpoint?

6. How does a person's belief about the Millennium impact his understanding of other portions of the Bible?

7. What is the difference between the premillennial and amillennial understanding of the Abrahamic Covenant?

8. Compare and contrast the Millennium with the new heaven and new earth.

Chapter Eight: Final Judgment

1. Explain the difference between the first resurrection and the second resurrection.

2. How is the first resurrection like a military parade (or carpool)?

3. When does the author believe that we who are living in the Church Age will receive our new bodies? How will our bodies differ from those of the Tribulation survivors during the Millennium?

4. Why will God release Satan at the end of the Millennium? Identify those whom Satan will deceive.

5. If someone were to ask you, "How do you know Christians cannot lose their salvation?" how would you respond?

6. Summarize the following about the Great White Throne Judgment:

    The participants in this judgment:
    The basis for this judgment:
    The result of this judgment:

7. Why will unbelievers be judged by their works at the Great White Throne Judgment?

Chapter Nine: Rewards in Heaven

1. Identify the participants at the Judgment Seat of Christ.

2. What makes this judgment different from the Great White Throne Judgment?

3. How would you answer someone who asked, "How could God judge me for my mistakes, since they have been forgiven by Christ?"

4. By what standards will Christians be evaluated at the Judgment Seat of Christ?

5. Can our good works earn God's approval? Explain.

6. What rewards can be earned at the Judgment Seat of Christ?

7. Describe the loss some Christians will suffer at the Judgment Seat of Christ.

8. As you reflect on this chapter, what specific changes could you make in your life right now to ensure future rewards?

Chapter Ten: The Truth about Eternity

1. What is the most common misconception people have about life after death?
2. What does Jesus' story about the rich man and Lazarus (Luke 16) reveal to us about hell?
3. How would you answer someone who said, "I don't believe a loving God would punish unbelievers forever"?
4. Why doesn't the Bible teach us more about heaven?
5. How do we know that heaven is an actual location rather than a state of mind?
6. Imagine you are speaking to a ten-year-old. Trace what happens to a Christian's spirit and body from the time he dies until the time of the new heaven and earth.
7. Why does the author believe we will recognize one another in heaven?
8. What aspect of heaven most appeals to you? Why?

NOTES

Chapter One: Why Study Bible Prophecy?

1. Paul Aurandt, *Paul Harvey's The Rest of the Story* (New York: Bantam Books, 1977), 43–45.

2. Billy Graham, speech at the Southern Baptist Convention, St. Louis, June 1987.

Chapter Two: It Begins and Ends with Israel

1. Henry Willen Van Loon, quoted in Russ Crosson, *A Life Well Spent* (Nashville: Thomas Nelson, 1994), 3.

Chapter Four: Not Left Behind

1. Charles C. Ryrie, *What You Should Know about the Rapture* (Chicago: Moody Press, 1981), 44.

2. Ibid., 28.

Chapter Five: When All Hell Breaks Loose

1. Aliza Marcus, "Jews, Muslims at Odds over Holy Shrine," *Wichita Falls Times Record News*, October 27, 1998, 3a.

2. Adapted from "Producing the Linen Garments of the Lay Priests for Service in the Temple," The Temple Institute, http://www.templeinstitute.org/garment _inauguration.htm#below.

3. J. Dwight Pentecost, *Things to Come: A Study in Biblical Eschatology* (Grand Rapids, MI: Zondervan, 1964), 246.

4. New Scientist staff and Reuters, "Mexicans get microchipped over kidnapping fears," *New Scientist,* August 22, 2008, http://www.newscientist.com/article /dn14589-mexicans-get-microchipped -over-kidnapping-fears.html.

5. Howard Amos, "Forty Russians Hospitalized After Meteorite Falls to Earth," The Guardian, February 15, 2013, http://www.theguardian.com/science/2013/feb/15/40-russians-hospitalised-after-meteorite-falls.

6. Adam Rogers, "Attention: Incoming Objects," Newsweek, March 24, 1997, 64.

7. My summary of the trumpet, seal, and bowl judgments is based, in part, on material from my former seminary professor, Dr. John Walvoord, and is explained in detail in his book, The Revelation of Jesus Christ (Chicago: Moody Press, 1966).

8. Adapted from Seth Robson, "U.S., Iraqi experts developing plan to preserve Babylon, build local tourism industry," Stars and Stripes, June 28, 2009, http://www.stripes.com/news/u-s-iraqi-experts-developing-plan-to-preserve-babylon-build-local-tourism-industry-1.92976.

Chapter Six: History's Most Important Event

1. William Martin, A Prophet with Honor (New York: William Morrow and Company, 1991), 281.

2. Federation of American Scientists, "Status of World Nuclear Forces," updated 2013, http://www.fas.org/programs/ssp/nukes/nuclearweapons/nukestatus.html.

3. Dean Babst and David Krieger, "Consequences of Using Nuclear Weapons," 1997, https://www.wagingpeace.org/articles/1997/00/00_babst_consequences.php.

4. Charles C. Ryrie, What You Should Know About the Rapture (Chicago: Moody Press, 1981), 43–46.

5. Michael P. Green, Illustrations for Biblical Preaching, (Grand Rapids, MI: Baker Book House, 1982), 434–35.

Chapter Seven: Heaven on Earth

1. "Dear Abby," The Dallas Morning News, January 15, 1991, 6c.

2. Charles Ryrie, The Basis for the Premillennial Faith (Neptune, NJ: Loizeaux Brothers Inc., 1953), 12.

3. Wolff Bachner, "What Lies Ahead for the State of Israel: An Interview with Dr. Manfred Gerstenfeld," April 19, 2013, http://www.inquisitr.com/625856/what-lies-ahead-for-the-state-of-israel-an-interview-with-dr-manfred-gerstenfeld/#GuO4LS18FgUQXT4H.99.

4. Ibid.

Chapter Eight: Final Judgment

1. Author's file, source unknown.
2. J. Dwight Pentecost, *Things to Come: A Study in Biblical Eschatology* (Grand Rapids, MI: Zondervan, 1964), 402.
3. Erwin W. Lutzer, *How You Can Be Sure That You Will Spend Eternity with God* (Chicago: Moody Press, 1996), 67–68.

Chapter Nine: Rewards in Heaven

1. Joe L. Wall, *Going for the Gold* (Chicago: Moody Press, 1991), 9–10.
2. Ibid., 87.
3. George F. Will, "The Gospel from Science," *Newsweek*, November 9, 1998, 88.
4. Robert Jeffress, *Say Goodbye to Regret* (Sisters, OR: Multnomah, 1998), 19–20.
5. Erwin W. Lutzer, *Your Eternal Reward* (Chicago: Moody Press, 1998), 80.

Chapter Ten: The Truth about Eternity

1. Harold Kushner, *When All You've Ever Wanted Isn't Enough* (New York: Simon and Schuster, 1986), 156–57.
2. Rob Bell, *Love Wins* (New York: HarperCollins, 2011), 170.
3. Robert Ingersoll, quoted in Billy Graham, *Facing Death* (Waco, TX: Word, 1987), 36.
4. J. Dwight Pentecost, *Things to Come: A Study in Biblical Eschatology* (Grand Rapids, MI: Zondervan, 1964), 555–60.
5. John Thomas, "That Hideous Doctrine," *Moody Monthly*, September 1985, 92.
6. Bell, *Love Wins*, 91.
7. Ibid., 108.
8. Randy Alcorn, *If God Is Good*, 319.
9. Thomas, "That Hideous Doctrine," 92.
10. "Hell's Sober Comeback," *U.S. News and World Report*, March 25, 1991, 56.
11. Charles Allen, *When You Lose a Loved One* (Westwood, NJ: Fleming H. Revell, 1959), 57–58.
12. W. A. Criswell and Paige Patterson, *Heaven* (Wheaton, IL: Tyndale House, 1991), 5–6.

13. W. A. Criswell, *Expository Sermons on Revelation* (Grand Rapids, MI: Zondervan, 1969), 129.

14. C. S. Lewis, *Mere Christianity*, C. S. Lewis Signature Series, rev. and exp. (HarperSanFrancisco, 2009), 226–27.

ABOUT THE AUTHOR

Dr. Robert Jeffress (DMin, Southwestern Theological Seminary; ThM, Dallas Theological Seminary) is an author and the senior pastor of the eleven-thousand-member First Baptist Church of Dallas, Texas. His bold, biblical, and practical ministry has made him one of the country's most respected evangelical leaders and earned him a Daniel Award from Vision America. He regularly appears on major mainstream media outlets such as Fox News, CNN, MSNBC, *The O'Reilly Factor*, *Cavuto on Business*, ABC's *Good Morning America*, and CBS's *The Early Show*. Dr. Jeffress is also the Bible teacher on *Pathway to Victory*, which airs daily on 764 radio stations nationwide and weekly on 1,200 television stations and cable systems, as well as 28 countries around the world.

If you liked this book, you'll love these!

TWIGHLIGHT'S LAST GLEAMING

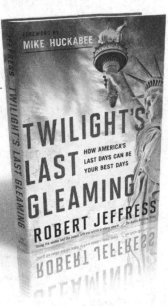

As the sun sets on a once-great nation, American Christians face a vital question: What Now?

Rarely in U.S. History have Christians been more discouraged and fearful about our country's future. Now Dr. Jeffress points a way out of this malaise, calling believers to action – not to restore a fading empire's glory, but to make an eternal impact on millions of eternal souls.

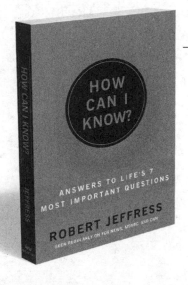

HOW CAN I KNOW?

It's okay to have questions. But you need answers you can trust."

— "How can I know there is a God?"
— "How can I know the Bible is true?"
— "How can I know there is life after death?"
— "How can I know how to forgive someone who has hurt me?"

In *How Can I Know?* Dr. Robert Jeffress tackles the seven most common and consequential of these questions and makes a compelling case for answers you can embrace with confidence.

AVAILABLE WHEREVER BOOKS ARE SOLD

How can I share
How Can I Know?

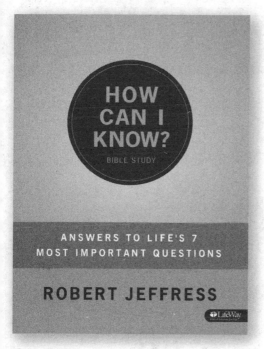

If you'd like to share the ideas from this book with your group, a video-driven Bible study is now available.

Stimulate deep discussion by bringing Dr. Jeffress right into the middle of your group setting through his video teaching. And inspire personal study five days a week with the devotionals included in the *Member Book*.

The contents of this study will compel your group to take action and live out their faith in everyday practical life experiences. Learn more online, call 800.458.2772, or visit the LifeWay Christian Store serving you.

lifeway.com/howcaniknow

IF YOU ENJOYED THIS BOOK, WILL YOU CONSIDER SHARING THE MESSAGE WITH OTHERS?

Mention the book in a blog post or through Facebook, Twitter, Pinterest, or upload a picture through Instagram.

Recommend this book to those in your small group, book club, workplace, and classes.

Head over to facebook.com/DrJeffress, "LIKE" the page, and post a comment as to what you enjoyed the most.

Tweet "I recommend reading #PerfectEnding by @RobertJeffress // @worthypub"

Pick up a copy for someone you know who would be challenged and encouraged by this message.

Write a book review online.

Visit us at worthypublishing.com

twitter.com/worthypub

worthypub.tumblr.com

facebook.com/worthypublishing

pinterest.com/worthypub

instagram.com/worthypub

youtube.com/worthypublishing